Dream It.
List It.

Do It!

How to Live a
Bigger & Bolder Life, from
the Life List Experts at
43Things.com

with Lia Steakley

Workman Publishing, New York

Library of Congress Cataloging-in-Publication Data
is available.

ISBN 978-0-7611-5126-5

Workman books are available at special discounts when
purchased in bulk for premiums and sales promotions
as well as for fund-raising or educational use.
Special editions or book excerpts can also be created
to specification. For details, contact the Special Sales Director
at the address below.

Cover and interior design by
Francesca Messina

Workman Publishing Company, Inc.
225 Varick Street
New York, NY 10014-4381
www.workman.com

Printed in the United States of America

First printing November 2008
10 9 8 7 6 5 4 3 2 1

Acknowledgments

The Robot Co-Op (the folks behind 43 Things) thanks the over 1.5 million users who made 43Things.com what it is today—you have contributed to the community that made this book and 43Things.com a reality. You rock.

Lia thanks the 43Things.com members for courageously pursuing the possibilities, sharing their life goals and achievements, and continually proving that listing your dreams is the best way to do it; her husband, Russell, for assisting in accomplishing a monumental goal on her life list (write a book . . . check); and The Robot Co-Op for viewing life as a grand experiment rather than a perfunctory formula.

We would like to thank the visionary team at Workman Publishing for recognizing the passion of the 43Things.com community and expertly translating it into a new medium. Special thanks to our editor, Maisie Tivnan, whose incisive editing made this book better in hundreds of ways, large and small; Michael Miller for mining the depths of 43Things.com for more inspiring goals and stories; Matthew Benjamin for getting the ball rolling; and Ruth Sullivan for her patience, wisdom, and guidance.

43 Chapters
for Your 43 Things

A Message from

43 Things

Remember your third grade self?

One thing you really had going for you was an unrestricted imagination. When people asked (and they often did), "What do you want to be when you grow up?" you had a ready answer. Sometimes more than one. Back then, your response could change daily—and wildly—from veterinarian to talk show host to astronaut. **There were no limits to your imagined future or to the many things you could be and do.**

Somewhere along the line, the focus of our dreams downshifts from what's imaginable to what's attainable—from what's fun to what's practical, from what's risky to what's responsible. Ambitions of playing in the NFL are dulled by playing (and losing) intramural college games, the desire to learn how to fly never gets off the ground, and aspirations to become a painter are put on hold for a job that pays. Life goes on, but not necessarily in the direction you had hoped. Or it goes on so predictably that you forget what it was like to imagine the unimaginable for yourself. You forget how to dream.

The idea of a life list is simple. What is it that you'd like to do but haven't taken the time or had the motivation to do? Bike across the country? Achieve enlightenment? Go skinny-dipping? Build a house with Habitat for Humanity? We believe that the very act of writing ideas down helps you answer the question **"What do I *really* want to do with my life?"** and puts you on the path toward accomplishing it. Creating a list—with the serious intent of checking things off—gives focus to dreams, defeats self-imposed limitations, and motivates you to achieve goals that once seemed lofty or unrealistic.

Sharing that list with others is just as powerful. Going public holds you accountable and connects you to new networks of serendipitous support. It was this very idea that inspired 43 Things. The website was started by three friends who wanted to form a company that could make our lives and the lives of others more meaningful. After trading paper lists of our goals, we concluded that a life list is a great way to communicate with and support each other, and so 43Things.com was born. The site helps you create your life list and then share your goals with more than 1.5 million other users.

Since its inception, 43Things.com has grown into an online encyclopedia of more than 1.3 million goals contributed by users from around the world. *Dream It. List It. Do It!* draws from the most interesting and inspiring of these goals to give you the broadest spectrum of life-changing possibilities and organizes them into 43 categories ranging from "Ignite Change" and "Be Silly" to "Fix My Finances" and "Do Something Daring." Sometimes it's just fun to see what other people dream about, not to mention what goals many of us have in common. (We've boldfaceed some of the most popular goals on the site.)

In addition, the book is packed with helpful, practical advice on how to accomplish hundreds of different goals and connects you directly to the resources you need. But perhaps even more valuable are the first-person stories from 43 Things members—ordinary people who have challenged themselves to dream big. Throughout the book you'll read inspiring accounts from individuals who made their dreams come true, whether by **hiking the Grand Canyon, becoming debt free, recording their own songs, or swimming in a bioluminescent bay.** Hearing from others who've completed some of the same goals that you want to accomplish is a great way to get motivated. You see that others can do it—and if they can do it, so can you. *Dream It. List It. Do It!* is person-to-person, do-it-yourself self-help for living a bigger and bolder life.

And we should know. Surrounded by such stories, we've been inspired to work on our own life lists. One of us has gone on tour with his band. Another has opened a bar. Another lost over 100 pounds. And we all decided to work four days a week to have more time to spend with family and friends. In the process of honing our life lists we've come up with something we call "Ten Rules for Creating and Conquering Your Life List" (see opposite page). These guidelines will help keep you focused and checking off your goals at a steady clip—as well as keep you from getting overwhelmed.

So nobody asks what you want to be when you grow up anymore, but you should never stop asking yourself what *you* want to do with your life. The answer to this question may change over the years and never be answered definitively. But that's part of the fun. Assume an "anything goes" attitude; suspend financial, geographical, and other limitations; and use this book as a tool to focus more on how you want to live each day. Start adding to your life list and you'll be ready to answer another important question: "What happens next?"

The team behind 43 Things
(Buster, Daniel, Ivan, Josh,
Laurel, Michelle, and Todd)

Ten Rules for Creating and Conquering Your Life List

1. Make your list public. Making your goals public solidifies your commitment to them, holds you accountable, and helps you connect with others who share your interests. You'll discover connections to social and professional networks that you didn't know you had and gets lots of encouragement from the people who care most about you. So make sure to tell friends, family members, and coworkers about your list and post it on the Internet at 43Things.com.

2. Include serious and fun goals. Vary the scope of your goals and include some wild just-for-fun dreams. Also, don't be afraid to complete less daunting goals first. Building momentum from these early successes helps you find the courage to tackle larger tasks.

3. Include undefined goals. Avoid overlooking a developing passion or interest by fearlessly adding goals even if you can't totally articulate them. If you wake up one morning with the desire to create art, add it to the list. Let the idea simmer in your mind until something more specific emerges.

4. Document progress. While reviewing the list, record your progress and determine the next steps. Documenting progress allows you to identify behavior patterns or other obstacles keeping you from accomplishing goals—it can also show you how far you've come.

5. Make goals manageable but rewarding. Divide big goals into smaller tasks, but not so small that they become tedious. Taking incremental steps keeps you from getting overwhelmed by a monumental goal. For example, instead of vowing to "get organized" try listing "declutter the garage."

6. Define the finish line. You'll find it easier to complete certain tasks and track progress if you determine the duration, results, or final outcome you desire from achieving a specific goal. Revise vague goals such as "give back to my community" by specifying what kind of work you want to do. You may not be able to do this right away—as we said, undefined goals are good, too.

7. Prioritize goals. Arrange your goals to reflect what you want to begin working on right away. You may want to run a marathon and get a promotion at work, but rather than trying to find the time and energy to run thirty miles a week *and* put in long hours at the office, focus on the goal that's more important to you.

8. Maintain a manageable list. Somewhere between twenty and forty-three is a sweet spot for many people. Limiting your life list to forty-three goals forces you to make some choices. Fewer than twenty goals doesn't offer enough variety to keep you moving forward.

9. Review your list weekly. It sharpens your focus, keeps up your momentum, and reminds you of what's important. As you review the list, ask yourself, "What have I done to achieve a particular goal this week?" If the answer is "nothing," is this goal important enough to keep on your list?

10. Revise and remove goals. A life list should be constantly evolving—it should reflect what's important to you *right now*, not what mattered in the past. Remember, there's no penalty for changing your mind or tweaking a goal to better reflect your desired outcome or new circumstances. A short-lived passion for making pottery can be reborn as "find a creative outlet," or ambitions to get straight A's in chemistry can be tossed because sometimes a passing grade is enough of a victory.

1

"Knowing others is wisdom, knowing yourself is enlightenment." —*Lao Tzu, philosopher*

Understand Myself

Early Christians laid massive tile labyrinths on their church floors to facilitate self-reflection and prayer. Walking a path from the outer edge of the maze to a single point in the center gave worshippers a physical manifestation of the meditative process of reaching their own centers. "Walking the labyrinth" is a good way to think about the journey inward. Understanding yourself is a long and elaborate process that often takes a circuitous route. The goal should not be to figure it out all at once but to examine patterns, assess bad habits, discover strengths, and come to terms with yourself by finding a way to embrace your flaws. Whether you look to tea leaves or a Jungian analyst, make it a priority to figure out what makes you tick and make peace with whatever that might be.

1

- ❏ Admit when I'm lying to myself
- ❏ Figure out what makes me truly happy

✪ Believe in myself

- ❏ Identify my strengths
- ❏ Remind myself, daily, that I matter
- ❏ Write in a "mood diary"
- ❏ Figure out why I procrastinate
- ❏ Analyze my dreams
- ❏ Find my passions
- ❏ Take 365 days of self-portraits

✪ Come to terms with my anger

- ❏ Figure out why I am single
- ❏ Come to terms with my past
- ❏ Read my horoscope daily

✪ Go to therapy

- ❏ Define my core values
- ❏ Come to terms with getting older
- ❏ Figure out why I fall in love with everyone
- ❏ Understand my parents
- ❏ Love myself
- ❏ Trace my family tree back at least six generations
- ❏ Decide for myself what is normal and what is not

"I like who I am."

This is what I know: I am a human, I have human reactions, I'm selfish and flawed and a perfectionist. I can work to limit my flaws, but I will always have some. And what's cool is that I really like myself and my craziness and all my flaws, and I understand my actions, feelings, and reactions.   —S.C.

❏ Understand why I do what I do
✪ **Be proud of myself**
❏ Define my likes and dislikes
❏ Write down my thoughts
❏ Understand my fears
❏ Come to terms with my sexuality
✪ **Accept myself**
❏ Soul search
❏ Decide which path I want to take
❏ Figure out what motivates me
❏ Understand the world around me
❏ Read all my old journals in chronological order
❏ Redefine, reconnect, and embrace the person I'm becoming
❏ Find out why I'm no good at relationships

Take a personality test

Although every person experiences the world differently, according to the well-known Myers-Briggs Type Indicator, you and everyone else can be described using sixteen psychological types. The test draws on the typological theories of Swiss psychiatrist Carl Jung and asks a series of questions about how you receive and process information. Complete the questionnaire at www.myersbriggs.org to assess your attitudes, approach to decision-making, level of empathy, and preference for relying on logic or emotions. Your score will indicate how your psychological type can help or hinder you and how to work or connect with those with opposite psychological characteristics.

❑ Understand that I know nothing
❑ Choose a theme song for myself
❑ Understand what I'm looking for in a mate
❑ Figure out what I need
✪ **Discover myself**
❑ Understand what religion means to me
❑ Decide if I want kids
❑ Know when to stand my ground, when to let things slide, and when to meet halfway

❑ Learn about my past lives
❑ Understand my mother
❑ Figure out if we should get married or not
❑ Decide if medication is right for me
✪ **Figure out what I believe**
❑ Keep a dream journal
❑ Come to terms with my adoption
❑ Read tea leaves

"In my opinion, loving yourself is . . ."

- accepting who you are
- acknowledging that your past is a part of you that you can't change, only learn from and use as an opportunity to grow
- accepting that you are human and not perfect, someone who makes mistakes and learns from them
- knowing that you deserve to be loved and acknowledging the need to love, too
- making the most of your natural beauty, talents, and skills; sharing them with others; and nurturing these aspects of yourself.

—G. E.

- ❏ Figure out if I love her
- ❏ Have my handwriting analyzed
- ❏ Figure out my priorities
- ❏ Understand how others perceive me

✪ **Find my purpose in life**

- ❏ Better understand my limitations
- ❏ Recognize how my words affect others
- ❏ Figure out why I'm so exhausted
- ❏ Learn to understand my own feelings
- ❏ Eliminate the stuff from my life that doesn't fulfill me spiritually, emotionally, or creatively
- ❏ Learn more about my subconcious mind
- ❏ Have a phrenology reading
- ❏ Understand my role as a stay-at-home mom
- ❏ Uncover what's really making me so anxious
- ❏ Find out what makes me tick
- ❏ Understand my kids better

✪ **Find my talent**

- ❏ Determine my political affiliations
- ❏ Understand why people dislike me
- ❏ Come to terms with my mortality
- ❏ Accept my failures
- ❏ Understand that some things are beyond my control

Understand your dreams

Some people believe that dreams are windows to your soul. Dreams provide a direct line to your subconscious, and interpreting them can be a powerful tool in understanding yourself on a nonrational level. Each night you dream for about 100 minutes, but remembering important details can be tricky, so document dreams in a bedside journal soon after waking. These tactics may help:

- Wake up slowly. Turn off your alarm and spend a minute or two lying motionless in bed before getting up.
- Focus on any residual memory of a dream, even if it's just a feeling or sensation of joy, sadness, or fear.
- Concentrate on locations, people, or other details, and replay these images in an effort to conjure up more of the dream.
- When you've brought as much as possible to mind, write down everything you can remember in your journal.
- Before you fall asleep at night, remind yourself to remember your dreams. Seems crazy, but it can help!

Check out www.dreamdoctor.com to help you figure out what it all means.

- ☐ Accept the fact that I am lonely, and do something about it
- ☐ Identify 10 strengths I am proud of
- ✪ **Figure out what I want to do with my life**
- ☐ Understand why I attach myself to unavailable men
- ☐ Figure out why I get so depressed sometimes

Write a "This I Believe" essay

Most of us live according to some philosophical belief or code of ethics, but not everyone can articulate them. Can you? Try to write a "This I Believe" essay and find out. Based on a popular radio show from the 1950s, "This I Believe" challenges you to articulate, share, and discuss the beliefs that shape your daily life. Tens of thousands of three-minute essays have been written and read on public radio with authors as varied as Albert Einstein, cabdrivers, and college students. Even if you don't get to read your essay on the air, making this a goal is great motivation to put pen to paper. You may discover that trying to explain your beliefs to others reveals things about yourself you never knew. Share your essay at www.thisibelieve.org.

> ## "I accept my achievements."
>
> I always feel the need to achieve at or above the level of my cohort. I feel like an underachieving bum if I'm not where I "should be" at a particular stage. Who am I racing against? Why am I running? What's the prize? I have no clue. I'm going to make the commitment to myself to accept my achievements for what they are. Life is not a race. I can go at my own pace.
>
> —R. E.

- ❏ Understand how the human brain works
- ⊙ **Compile a list of 100 facts about myself**
- ❏ Visit all the places I used to live
- ❏ Discover what *I* like rather than what people *tell* me to like
- ❏ Make a list of my family's shared personality traits
- ❏ Understand my sexual desires
- ❏ Lose myself, then find myself all over again

2

"I want to keep a childlike sense of wonder about the world. That way I will appreciate whatever I see, taste, smell, hear, or feel. There is always something new to learn, always something wonderful to discover and explore."

—*M.L., 43 Things member*

Learn New Things

Children have an innate curiosity about the world. They're always asking "Why?" and "How come?" and questioning things you stopped wondering about a long time ago (like "Why does a leopard have spots?" or "How come I have ten toes?"). Kids have the right idea. It's time to recapture some of that youthful curiosity by learning something new every day, every week, or just every once in a while. Learning new things isn't about getting smarter, it's about being interested (*and* more interesting). So enlist a friend to school you in the art of juggling, ask an aunt to teach you the rules of bridge, or buy a book on the solar system. You can learn anywhere, at any time, as long as you keep your mind, your eyes, and your ears wide open.

✪ **Never lose my sense of wonder**
- ❏ Learn to drive a stick shift
- ❏ Learn the art of bonsai

✪ **Learn self-hypnosis**
- ❏ Learn to cook Indian food
- ❏ Learn to identify the constellations
- ❏ Learn how to hand-bind books
- ❏ Learn how to apply makeup
- ❏ Learn to do a handstand
- ❏ Learn to fly a helicopter
- ❏ Learn to swim
- ❏ Learn secret spy skills
- ❏ Learn how to deal with difficult people
- ❏ Learn tricks on a flying trapeze
- ❏ Learn to whistle with my fingers
- ❏ Learn from my mistakes
- ❏ Learn tai chi
- ❏ Learn how to tie the stem of a maraschino cherry with my tongue
- ❏ Learn how to make a great cup of coffee

✪ **Learn to skateboard**
- ❏ Learn how to roll my Rs
- ❏ Learn more about botany
- ❏ Learn to throw knives

"I learned blacksmithing."

Some fifteen years after catching my first whiff of soft coal burning, I completed my first blacksmithing course. Before taking the beginner's blacksmithing class, I hadn't so much as walked through a metal shop. But I learned to forge, weld pieces together, make curves and twists, split metal, and, of course, how not to maim myself. By the end, I had several coat hooks, a decorative wrought-iron heart, and barbecue forks, plus a number of small cuts and burns on my hands and a burning desire to continue blacksmithing.

Once you get the chance to beat on an anvil for a few hours, you will never look at a chunk of metal the same way again. Things normally considered trash, like broken wrenches or pieces of steel, find a second life in the forge. If you get the chance to talk or work with a blacksmith, do so. Take notes, buy a forge, hammer, anvil, and tongs on the cheap and try out a few ideas. It will change your outlook on a lot of things, like why buy when you can build? — S. K.

❑ Learn calligraphy
✪ **Learn to drive**
❑ Learn to shoot a gun

Learn something new every day

You can learn anywhere—your car during your daily commute, your couch at 2 A.M., and your desk first thing in the morning. Try some of these:

- Tune into public radio stations and transform your car into a classroom during daily commutes. Local stations work hard to come up with diverse programming that gives you not only news, but also smart shows on science, the arts, and health. You can also listen to audiobooks or learn a language by listening to CDs.

- The boob tube can actually be a great teacher: Try watching the History Channel, PBS, and the Discovery Channel. From original footage of D-Day to stories on code breakers and lost ancient civilizations or profiles of icons from Beethoven to Jimi Hendrix, you can finally justify those hours on the couch.

- Start each morning with an e-mail from Fact Me! (www.factme.com) that gives you unusual facts, such as the origin of the phrase "It's raining cats and dogs" and how fast atoms travel, or learn a new word a day by subscribing to Wordsmith's free daily e-mail (www.wordsmith.org/awad/).

❑ Learn Zen archery

❑ Learn how to kiss better

❑ Learn to weave fabric

✪ **Learn sign language**

❑ Learn to roller skate

❑ Learn how to make small talk with strangers

❑ Learn to yodel

❑ Learn numerology

✪ **Learn French**

❑ Learn silk screening

❑ Learn to wrestle

❑ Learn to ride a motorcycle

❑ Learn to be ambidextrous

❑ Learn silversmithing

❑ Learn to sew with a sewing machine

❑ Learn how to wallpaper a room

❑ Learn to wink

❑ Learn to moonwalk

✪ **Learn to bartend**

❑ Learn acupuncture

❑ Learn some basic carpentry skills

❑ Learn to purr

❑ Learn astrology

✪ **Learn to do a cartwheel**

- ❑ Learn to rock climb
- ❑ Learn taxidermy
- ✪ **Learn Hebrew**
- ❑ Learn falconry
- ❑ Learn to figure skate
- ❑ Learn to throw a pot
- ❑ Learn to read Braille
- ❑ Learn how to play backgammon
- ❑ Learn to ride a unicycle
- ✪ **Learn a magic trick**
- ❑ Learn to wakeboard
- ❑ Learn about local politics
- ❑ Learn more about mythology
- ❑ Learn to speak fluent gibberish
- ❑ Learn to draw
- ❑ Learn to be a storyteller

"I learned how to snowboard."

The first day you'll spend on your butt. The second day you'll spend on your knees. And the third day it all comes together and you're going down the slopes. I'm fifty-six years old, live in Memphis, Tennessee, and I own three snowboards. Go rip it like there's no tomorrow!   —S. Y.

Learn CPR

Being trained in CPR could mean the difference between life and death in a medical emergency. Whether someone is drowning, choking, suffering a cardiac arrest, or simply not breathing, CPR extends the window of time a person can survive without oxygen (typically four minutes), until paramedics arrive. Learn skills to save a life by enrolling in a CPR course through the American Red Cross. Search for classes by ZIP code at www.redcross.org.

- ❑ Learn to practice homeopathy
- ❑ Learn the principles of feng shui
- ❑ Learn some smooth, cool dance moves
- ❑ Learn a new sport
- ✪ **Learn how to talk dirty**
- ❑ Learn how to invest in stocks
- ❑ Learn Shiatsu massage
- ❑ Learn watchmaking
- ❑ Learn to quilt
- ❑ Learn gymnastics
- ❑ Learn how to hot-wire a car
- ❑ Learn Arabic
- ❑ Learn swordsmanship

Learn origami

An ancient Japanese tradition, origami involves more than folding colorful paper into butterflies and frogs—each design and color contains a certain meaning. A green flower is a symbol of friendship, representing healing, strength, and balance. A crane represents honor and loyalty, and according to legend, anyone who folds a thousand origami cranes will be granted a wish such as a long life or recovery from illness. Make your next wish come true by visiting a nearby arts and crafts store or the online Origami Paper Store (www.origamipaperstore.com) for supplies. Learn to turn simple paper into unique gifts for friends and family with Margaret Van Sicklen's *The Joy of Origami* or *Beginning Origami* by Steve and Megumi Biddle.

❏ Learn more about Gandhi
❏ Learn reflexology
✪ **Learn how to play poker**
❏ Learn how to seduce
❏ Learn the art of mosaic making
❏ Learn to hacky sack
✪ **Learn to ride a horse**
❏ Learn something about everything

❏ Learn to fly-fish
❏ Learn how to play bridge
❏ Buy turntables and learn to deejay
✪ **Learn wood carving**
❏ Learn pinhole photography
❏ Learn how to do a jackknife off a high dive
❏ Learn shorthand
❏ Learn how to flirt
❏ Learn survival skills
❏ Learn how to snowshoe
❏ Learn how to do my own hair
❏ Learn about voodoo
✪ **Learn to water ski**
❏ Learn to tell fortunes
❏ Learn how to tattoo
❏ Learn to spot good antiques at yard sales
❏ Learn how to do a pushup
❏ Learn more about geography
❏ Learn Sanskrit
❏ Learn how to beatbox
✪ Learn how to rappel down a mountain
❏ Learn how to read hieroglyphics
✪ **Learn about forensics**
❏ Learn witchcraft

3

"It is only in adventure that some people succeed in knowing themselves—in finding themselves." —*André Gide*

Be More Adventurous

Throwing yourself out of a plane at 10,000 feet
in the air, trekking up an icy peak with nothing
but a rope and an ax, ingesting a spoonful of
cow brains—is this really the stuff dreams are
made of? If your answer is "Yes!" then you
should need no extra encouragement to read
on and add some more death-defying feats to
your life list. For those who are not daring by
nature, remember that being adventurous isn't
about chasing after death and trying to cheat it
in the end. It's about mustering the courage to
do something you never thought possible and
feeling more alive in one moment than you've
ever felt in a lifetime. The real thrill is in pushing
your limits and learning the liberating lesson
that there is *nothing* you're incapable of doing.

✪ Be fearless

- ❑ Go on an archaeology expedition of the underwater pyramids off the coast of Japan
- ❑ Eat grasshoppers in Thailand
- ❑ White water raft through the Grand Canyon
- ❑ Eat cow brains
- ❑ Parasail in the Andes

✪ Jump off a waterfall

- ❑ Walk across hot coals
- ❑ Free-climb a mountain
- ❑ Race the entire length of Route 66 with my friends
- ❑ Drive a monster truck
- ❑ Go underwater spelunking

✪ Climb Mount Kilimanjaro

- ❑ Helicopter ski
- ❑ Do an Outward Bound Wilderness course
- ❑ Trek through Tibet
- ❑ Start a fight club
- ❑ Take a 50-mile bike ride
- ❑ Swim across the Strait of Gibraltar
- ❑ Race motorcycles
- ❑ Surf on every continent's coastlines
- ❑ Parachute from a helicopter

Be More Adventurous

"I jumped out of a plane."

I was in this little plane. Squished. I felt like canned tuna.
It took forever to get up to 10,000 feet. Finally. Altitude
reached. Door opens. LOUD wind all around. I scooted on
my butt, the jumpmaster harnessed me to him, and we were
at the door. He shouted at me to put my foot on the step but
I couldn't. He ended up pushing us out of the plane.

The next few seconds were the most exhilarating seconds
of my life. I tumbled about, spinning, seeing clouds every
which way no matter which side was up. Everything was
still loud. Windy loud. Piercingly loud. Finally, the chute
opens, and I get yanked up. All of a sudden, it grew quiet.
I heard my jumpmaster say: "Congratulations, you just fell
7,000 feet." I laughed.   — B.N.L.

❑ Swing on a trapeze
✪ **BASE jump**
❑ Walk along the Great Wall of China
❑ Participate in a Polar Bear Club swim
❑ Scale the side of a cliff
❑ Camp in Death Valley
❑ Learn to rail slide on skis
❑ Participate in an Antarctic expedition

Dive to the *Titanic*

Travel to the bottom of the Atlantic Ocean in a submersible deep-dive vessel and be one of the few nonscientists to view this legendary shipwreck. Spend hours 2.5 miles below the surface navigating the decomposing (but still recognizable) stern and bow and surrounding debris from the RMS *Titanic* wreckage. The eleven-day trip includes meals, accommodations aboard the Russian research vessel *Akademik Mstislav Keldysh*, and a guided tour down through the icy deep to the *Titanic* grave site. Check out the Great Canadian Adventure Company (www.adventures.ca) for more information. This once-in-a-lifetime trip costs more than most of us can afford, but don't let that stop you from making it a goal.

- ❏ Sail through the Bermuda Triangle
- ❏ Compete in an amateur kickboxing tournament
- ❏ Tour rural Alaska in a helicopter
- ❏ Saddle break and train a horse
- ❏ Jump over a car on a motorcycle
- ✪ **Swim with sharks in a cage**
- ❏ Snowboard down an active volcano
- ❏ Participate in a camel race

❑ Land a 720-degree jump on skis
❑ Put $100 a month into an "adventure fund"
✪ **Chase a tornado**
❑ Drive in a demolition derby
❑ Ride a train across America
❑ Cross a desert in a pickup truck
❑ Go wingsuit flying

"I rode a bull."

When my bull was moved into the bucking chutes*, my heart started racing, and it felt like I had a brick in my stomach. I climbed up into the chutes and screwed down on the back of the bull. I wrapped my hand in the rope, turned my spurs in, and took a deep breath, thinking, "This is it." The chute slammed open and the bull blew out with a huge kick. At that point I wasn't scared anymore. My instincts had taken over—all I could do was bear down, grip with my spurs, and pull up on the rope.

When the buzzer sounded, I unwrapped my hand, rolled off the bull, and ran to the fence like my hair was on fire. When I got back behind the chutes, I felt a mix of pure euphoria and relief that the ride was over.   —W. C.

*The pen where riders mount bulls before being set loose into the arena.

- ☐ Dive with a whale shark
- ☐ Sail solo around the world
- ☐ Climb the Himalayas
- ☐ Eat a tequila worm
- ☐ Participate in a snowshoe race
- ☐ Climb Mount Everest
- ☐ Have adventures instead of relationships
- ☐ Skate in a roller-derby bout
- ✪ **Bungee jump**
- ☐ Race sled dogs in Alaska

Survive in the wilderness

High-tech camping gear has essentially rendered primitive survival skills unnecessary with one exception: building the perfect fire. Here's a surefire way:

1. Gather tinder (dry leaves, grass, or bark), kindling (small sticks or twigs), and larger logs.
2. Build a circle out of large rocks to serve as the fireplace.
3. In the circle, arrange sticks in the shape of a tepee over the pile of tinder, leaving enough space between them for good air circulation.
4. Ignite the kindling; as the sticks catch fire and fall, add larger pieces of wood in a similar tepee formation.

> ## "I climbed Aconcagua."
>
> It's an amazing experience to climb a mountain, especially one that is nearly 23,000 feet high. I'll never forget how bright and clear the stars are, or how amazing the sunsets are down there somewhere between Chile and Argentina. —W. W.

❑ Go ice climbing

❑ Race four-wheelers

❑ Swim the English Channel

❑ Travel the entire perimeter of South America on foot

❑ Dive into the ocean from a cliff

❑ Squat in an abandoned building

✪ **Risk failure**

❑ Go deep-sea fishing

❑ Play extreme Frisbee golf

❑ Deliver a baby in an emergency

❑ Mountain bike the Continental Divide

✪ **Live in the jungle**

❑ Do one thing a month that scares me

❑ Do three consecutive toe-ups on a trapeze with no spotter

❑ Free-fall more than 1,000 feet

Ride the world's fastest roller coasters

Ascend peaks measuring several hundred feet high and roar down them at speeds topping 100 miles per hour. A good roller coaster packs a heavy dose of adventure and adrenaline into a ride that lasts less than a minute. Here are the world's three fastest roller coasters to test your nerves:

- Kingda Ka, Six Flags Great Adventure, Jackson Township, New Jersey
- Top Thrill Dragster, Cedar Point, Sandusky, Ohio
- Dodonpa, Fuji-Q Highland, Fujiyoshida, Japan

❏ Dogsled at the Arctic Circle
❏ Water-ski behind a catamaran
❏ Join in a deep-sea exploration
❏ Walk across a tightrope
❏ Participate in a cryptozoological expedition
❏ Go king crabbing in Alaska
❁ **Travel faster than the speed of sound**
❏ Do a backflip on a BMX bike
❏ Swim across Lake Ontario
❏ Travel to uncharted territory
❏ Race in the Iditarod
❏ Saddle train a longhorn

✪ **Climb the Matterhorn**

❑ Hitch a ride with a stranger

❑ Hunt big game in Alaska

❑ Run the Canadian Death Race

❑ Go helicopter snowboarding

❑ Eat fire

❑ Charter a yacht and cruise the South Pacific

❑ Build a house with hidden rooms and
secret passageways

❑ Wrestle an alligator

❑ Be the hero of my own life story

❑ Live without a net

4

"That best portion of a good
   man's life,
His little, nameless,
   unremembered acts
Of kindness and of love."

—*William Wordsworth*

Make a Difference

Make a difference by leaving things a little better than you found them. A kind word or gesture goes a long way and often costs only a few minutes of your time. Hold the door open for someone whose hands are full, take an interest in others' lives, or offer hopeful words to those going through tough times. You'll discover that doing good deeds inspires people to follow your lead, so spark a ripple of goodwill by adopting goals to volunteer in your community, become a mentor, or just help a neighbor. Then challenge yourself to transform these random acts of kindness into a regular practice. And whenever it feels like you have nothing to offer, remember that even the smallest favor can affect someone's life in ways you could never anticipate.

✪ **Make people laugh**
- ❏ Help an elderly person cross the road
- ❏ Give away all my possessions
- ❏ Take a trip to a third world country with a missionary group
- ❏ Help troubled teens
- ❏ Organize a spa day for the residents of a battered women's shelter
- ❏ Pick up loose change and donate it to charity
- ❏ Call my representatives and make my opinion heard
- ❏ Become an organ donor
- ❏ Teach underprivileged children to play music
- ❏ Make dinner for the homeless guys out at the beach

✪ **Support local music**
- ❏ Pick up a four-leaf clover and give it to someone who really needs it
- ❏ Build an animal rescue sanctuary
- ❏ Volunteer as a family
- ❏ Pick up trash for a day
- ❏ Protest for a cause I believe in
- ❏ Have time and money to volunteer in social work

"I sponsor a child."

For the last two years, I've been sponsoring a child in Cambodia through Worldvision (www.worldvision.org). I write letters about three times a year to Theary, and she sends me pictures. Because of the sponsorship program, she gets a chance to go to school, have a school bag, wear shoes, and still have food on the table at home. Theary is very creative and loves to draw for me. She wants to be a teacher when she grows up. If the whole world would give a little, imagine what a better world it would be. —L. M.

❏ Send a donation to my college
✪ **Become a doctor to make a difference**
❏ Donate rice through FreeRice.com
❏ Volunteer as an HIV counselor
❏ Advocate for more vegetarian options on campus
❏ Raise money for the world's water crisis
❏ Buy stuff that's made in the USA
❏ Donate 20% of my paycheck to UNICEF
❏ Volunteer for a search-and-rescue team
❏ Save my fruit seeds and plant them in public spaces
❏ Be a volunteer grandparent
❏ Revitalize my downtown

Write to a prisoner

Inmates may have committed acts that you morally disagree with, but writing to people behind bars lets them know they are not without hope or the ability to make better choices. You can contact prisoners through websites such as www.writeaprisoner.com or www.prisonerlife.com. When writing to prisoners, keep the following tips in mind:

- Consider setting up a post office box to keep your home or work address confidential.
- Be respectful of inmates and up-front about your reason for contacting them and let them know how often you plan to send mail.
- Write about casual topics such as your interests, hobbies, favorite books, movies, sports teams, or current events, but don't include personal information.
- Send cards for holidays and the person's birthday, which can be particularly lonely.

❑ Attend a city council meeting
❑ Hand out flowers at a nursing home
✪ **Leave everything a little better than I found it**
❑ Buy more fair-trade products

- ❏ March for a cause
- ❏ Minister in a women's shelter
- ❏ Give a lottery ticket to a stranger
- ❏ Volunteer in an Eastern European orphanage
- ❏ Serve Christmas dinner at a homeless shelter
- ❏ Become a teacher
- ❏ Volunteer at a zoo
- ❏ Do a good deed once a day
- ❏ Make someone I care about happy
- ❏ Pay for the car behind me at the toll booth
- ❏ Rescue and rehabilitate racehorses
- ⊙ **Make someone else's dream come true**
- ❏ Volunteer at the orangutan sanctuary in Borneo
- ❏ Leave cookies in the mailbox for the mailman
- ❏ Volunteer at an orphanage in Thailand

"I donated my eggs."

Although donating is not for everyone, I have donated to two couples, and it has been the most amazing experience. These families are so hopeful and so dedicated to having children that you truly become an angel to them. Not only is it the most precious gift you can give, but it was also a way for me to pay for college. —B. D.

- ☐ Start a petition for a cause I care about
- ☐ Give love to those who are without it
- ☐ Donate toys to a children's hospital
- ☐ Put money in expired parking meters
- ☐ Go through my wardrobe and donate the things I'll never use again
- ✪ **Be a mental health advocate**
- ☐ Start a recovery house for addicts
- ☐ Give more compliments
- ☐ Raise money for Sudanese refugees
- ☐ Volunteer at a wildlife center
- ☐ Be an advocate for young single moms
- ☐ Help raise awareness about sweatshops
- ☐ Put on a benefit concert

"I try to change the world, twenty minutes at a time."

Yesterday, my neighbor across the street had a cardiac ablation to correct a severe arrhythmia problem, and even though it was a pretty serious surgery, it was done on an outpatient basis. She was back home in time for dinner, so I made dinner for her family. It may not have changed the whole world, but it made a nice difference in hers.   —Y. O.

Give someone a microloan

Help entrepreneurs in the developing world start or grow businesses by providing loans of $25 or more through the micro-lending website Kiva. The process is simple: Go to www.kiva.org, search profiles describing entrepreneurs' businesses and reasons for requesting loans, choose an amount to invest, and receive repayment in monthly increments. Through the website, hundreds of thousands of entrepreneurs receive funding and improve their businesses and quality of life. In return, investors get updates about business owners' progress and the satisfaction of helping others achieve economic independence.

❑ Give something away every time I get something new
✪ **Smile at strangers**
❑ Run a community center
❑ Volunteer with the Red Cross
❑ Be an anonymous donor
❑ Participate in a beach cleanup
❑ Rescue and give love to stray animals
❑ Make a difference in the lives of my students
❑ Bring blankets to homeless people

Build a house with Habitat for Humanity

Spend a few hours or a weekend building homes with Habitat for Humanity. Even if you've never held a hammer, you can still be a useful volunteer. Habitat for Humanity offers programs geared to teaching women and youth construction skills; volunteers receive instruction and guidance from professionals at building sites, and you can always work on simple tasks to ready homes before the move-in date. Join projects in your community or around the globe by searching the database of volunteer opportunities at www.habitat.org.

❑ Start a program to help inner-city kids
❑ Register underrepresented voters
❑ Sing at a nursing home
❑ Raise money for Parkinson's disease research
❑ Knit chemo caps for charity
✪ **Give blood**
❑ Raise awareness about domestic violence
❑ Advocate for animals
❑ Donate books to the public library
❑ Raise money for multiple sclerosis research

Make a **Difference**

- ❑ Establish a camp for at-risk children and teens
- ❑ Volunteer for Lifeline
- ❑ Coordinate a fashion show to benefit a charity
- ❑ Volunteer at the Ronald McDonald House
- ❑ Promote body acceptance at my school
- ❑ Help someone whose car has broken down on the side of the road
- ❑ Raise awareness for organ donation
- ❑ Volunteer at the library
- ✪ **Write a letter to the editor**
- ❑ Raise money for breast cancer research
- ❑ Save the whales
- ❑ Work to enforce legislation I believe in
- ❑ Donate winter coats for kids
- ❑ Advocate for the Great Ape Project
- ❑ Be the change I want to see in the world

5

"Too many people don't like looking at their finances because it makes them feel bad. But they're *your* finances—you're the only person they'll affect and you're the only person who can fix them."

—*R.N., 43 Things member*

Fix My Finances

Let's face it. Your plan to win the lottery is not a realistic personal-finance strategy. We all want to be standing on a solid financial foundation, but for many of us, that foundation is more like a quivering mound of Jell-O. More than a quarter of Americans live from paycheck to paycheck; 43 percent of households have $1,000 or less in savings; and 60 percent of us don't pay our credit card balances each month. Does the thought of your student debt and the cost of your daily lattes make you want to dive under the covers? It shouldn't. Facing your financial fears can pay off big. Summon the courage to track monthly expenses, balance your checkbook, and finally answer the question, "Where does all my money go?" Then *consciously decide* where you want it to go instead.

✪ **Contribute more to my 401K**
- ❑ Consolidate my credit card debt
- ❑ Become an expert thrift-store shopper
- ❑ Pay my taxes
- ❑ Move to a cheaper city and get more for my money
- ❑ Invest in a mutual fund
- ❑ Buy an investment property
- ❑ Read more books on retirement options
- ❑ Stick to a budget
- ❑ Get a loan

✪ **Talk to a financial planner**
- ❑ Put a dollar a day into a piggy bank
- ❑ Eat out less
- ❑ Track how much I spend and what I spend it on
- ❑ Open a money market account
- ❑ Pay off my mortgage
- ❑ Start a new savings account
- ❑ Invest in vineyards
- ❑ Switch to a bank that doesn't have ATM fees

✪ **Stop impulse shopping**
- ❑ Save for my wedding
- ❑ Invest (rather than spend) my tax refund

"I paid off all of my student loans."

I paid off that horrible monster called student debt by denying myself lunches out and learning to find fun for free (or under a $10 limit). I socked away Christmas, birthday, and Easter money from relatives, and when the $10,000 goal came near, I celebrated. When the $5,000 goal came near, I celebrated. Then when the $2,500 goal came near, I cried. When I finally paid off this nightmare, I celebrated by moving out of the country—something I'd wanted to do for years.   —M. K.

❑ Pay my rent on time
❑ Hold a yard sale and use the money to pay off my credit cards
❑ Invest in alternative energy
❑ Pay back my parents
❑ Save for college
❑ Get a second (or third) job
❍ **Start investing in the stock market**
❑ Buy an apartment
❑ Grow my own vegetables and herbs and avoid the supermarket at all costs

Build a rainy day fund

Everyone should have an emergency savings account that holds enough money to live for six months. Begin by assessing your monthly expenses. Then create a savings strategy, such as trimming 10 percent of all expenses, which lowers the amount you need to save, and funnel the money into a designated account. Pinch pennies by taking lunch to work, using a water bottle instead of bottled water, and clipping coupons. Eliminating minor expenses and saving as little as $2.80 per day nets an extra $1,000 a year. The important thing is to *get started*.

❑ Invest in gold
✪ **Stop using shopping as therapy**
❑ Put money into my IRA every month
❑ Support my family
❑ Improve my credit score
❑ Sort out back pay owed to me
❑ Pack lunch instead of buying it
❑ Save money to travel abroad
✪ **Help my parents retire**
❑ Pay for my great-great-great-great-grandchildren's education

❑ Invest 10% of my salary each month

❑ Become financially independent so I can do what
I want, when I want

✪ **Use coupons every week**

❑ Find ways to make my huge mortgage payments
less onerous and scary

❑ Develop a money management system

❑ Make enough money so my spouse and I can
retire early

✪ **Join an investment club**

❑ Get a job that will make me big (enough) bucks

❑ Go to the gym regularly or cancel my membership

"I set financial challenges for myself."

What I did to complete this goal:

■ Bought no magazines for a month—a very, very hard
thing for me to do, but I was strong

■ Bought no vending machine snacks this month and was
able to save more than $50 in change!

■ Put $100 in savings

■ Lowered my light bill even more than the goal I had set
(amazing!) —C. D.

Be smart about your credit cards

As anyone who has struggled to pay down credit card debt will tell you, interest compounds much more quickly than the rewards companies offer. Reduce or eliminate your dependency on credit cards with these tips:

- Use what's called a secured credit card—a card preloaded with a cash balance, so that you make interest-free purchases.
- Don't wait for the bill to arrive in the mail. Online banking tools make it easy for you to pay off your credit card weekly. This will help you avoid late payments as well as keep on top of your spending.
- Lock up your cards and use them only in specific transactions requiring a credit card, such as reserving a hotel room, renting a car, or buying airline tickets online.
- If your credit cards continue to get the best of you each month, cancel them, pay for everything with cash, and use a PayPal account for online purchases.

❑ Invest more aggressively
❑ Buy a condo
❑ Calculate an annual budget

- ❏ Cancel my cable subscription
- ❏ Find a job
- ❏ Never buy things at full price
- ❏ Get lower-interest credit cards
- ❏ Manage my portfolio more closely
- ✪ **Get out of debt and stay out of debt**
- ❏ Quit gambling
- ❏ Set up automatic deposits from my checking account to my savings account
- ❏ Save up for a house
- ✪ **Get rich quick**
- ❏ Stay away from shopping malls
- ❏ Make an appointment with a certified financial planner
- ❏ Limit gift purchases to $20
- ❏ Consolidate my credit cards
- ❏ Find a cheaper cell phone plan
- ❏ Save enough money for an engagement ring
- ❏ Open a holiday savings account
- ❏ Set up direct deposit with my employer
- ❏ Pick up more shifts at work
- ❏ Go to the library instead of buying new books
- ✪ **Live within my means**
- ❏ Put money in a savings account and forget it exists

> ## "I'm saving for retirement."
>
> Open a Roth IRA. The earlier in life you start your IRA, the
> bigger the snowball will get as it keeps rolling. The key to
> this is compounding. Put the money in while you're 20, 25,
> 30, and you'll have a huge wad o' cash to fall back on later
> in life—don't put it off.   —M. D.

- ❏ Set up mutual funds for the kids in my life
- ❏ Research my employer's retirement plan options
- ❏ Win the lottery
- ❏ Start an investing club for women
- ❏ Double the amount in my savings account
- ❏ Save money for my kids to go to college
- ✪ **Never use a credit card again**
- ❏ Work more hours
- ❏ Entertain company at home instead of going out
- ❏ Save up enough money so that not working becomes an option
- ✪ **Care less about material possessions**
- ❏ Find a cheaper apartment
- ❏ Develop a bill-filing system

❏ Balance my checkbook and stop overdrawing my checking account
❏ Clear up the mistakes on my credit report
❏ Have more money coming in than going out
❏ Get a business loan
❏ Track everything I spend for a week
❏ Become a billionaire
❏ Keep abreast of financial news
❏ Have time and money to volunteer
❏ Rebuild my savings account
❏ Stop using payday loans
✪ **Get a raise**
❏ Find an interest-free loan to pay for school
❏ Take a course in personal investing
❏ Pay off my credit card . . . again
✪ **Consolidate my loans**
❏ Save up for a laptop
❏ Make enough money with my artwork so that I can quit my job
❏ Don't be afraid to open my bills as soon as they arrive
❏ Pay off my home loan
❏ Find a roommate to help with rent
❏ Pay my parking tickets

Draw up a budget

A budget is an essential step in reaching financial independence—knowing what you can afford to spend is the only way to know how to save.

- Organize expenses into essential and nonessential spending. (If you're not sure where your $250 dye jobs fall, ask yourself: Does this contribute to my long-term goals or survival?) Break down vague groups such as "entertainment" into books, movies, CDs, etc.

- Track expenses for a month using financial software such as Microsoft Money or Quicken, or by saving all receipts for thirty days and keeping a daily spending notebook or spreadsheet.

- Add up all your expenses, subtract the total from your income after taxes, and take a deep breath.

- Figure out where you can cut back on spending until your monthly income and expenses are equal or, better yet, your income is larger.

- Give yourself a weekly allowance for pocket money. Each week withdraw that amount in cash and use it to pay for small nonbudgeted expenses. When the cash is gone, the spending stops. Period. No exceptions.

❑ Create a healthy cash buffer
❑ Sell my car and ride the bus
✪ **Stop living paycheck to paycheck**
❑ Start piggybank saving again
❑ Hold a clothing swap
❑ Spend less when going out for drinks
❑ Have multiple streams of passive income
❑ Have a garage sale
❑ Sell my things on eBay
❑ Live within 80% of my income
❑ Buy a rental property
✪ **Make ethical investments**
❑ Research lower car insurance options
❑ Cut my monthly expenses by 10%

6

"Catch, then, oh catch
the transient hour;
Improve each moment
as it flies!" —*Samuel Johnson*

Live in the Moment

Ever feel like you operate in only three modes:
rewind, play, and fast-forward? It's time to hit
pause and take a breath. Because as Ferris
Bueller, the king of carpe diem, once said,
"Life goes by pretty fast. If you don't stop and
look around once in a while, you could miss it."
So let go of past mistakes, stop stressing over
daily deadlines, and forget your fears about
the future. You can look at life either as a series
of hours and minutes in which to accomplish
tasks, or as a series of moments and experiences
to be noticed, relished, and lived. Turn down the
volume on the noisy racket that is your daily
grind and cultivate the habit of enjoying life's
simpler gifts. Indulge in small pleasures and
you may find that the world doesn't spin quite
as fast as it used to.

- ☐ Smile at everyone who meets my eye
- ☐ Take a whole summer off, like a kid from school
- ☐ Fall asleep in a field of white daisies as someone reads me poetry
- ☐ Be daring and passionate, to hell with the consequences
- ☐ Sit under a tree and enjoy the fresh air
- ☐ Say yes to life
- ✪ **Live each day as if it were my last, but learn each day as if I'll live forever**
- ☐ Do something unexpected
- ☐ Start "Free Hug Fridays"
- ☐ Leave heads-up pennies for others to find

Go for a midnight picnic

Practice serendipity and invite someone to the rooftop or lawn for an impromptu midnight picnic. Gather snacks, beverages, flashlights or candles, and a blanket. Don't overthink the menu, just grab an assortment of goodies found in pantries, refrigerators, and all-night convenience stores. The magic and romance of an al fresco midnight snack should make up for the lack of gourmet treats.

"I dance in the rain."

I love the rain! Nothing makes me feel more alive, happy, and in the moment than dancing in a heavy rainfall. My roommates were dumbfounded once when I went from lounging in the living room watching a movie, to running outside during a cold April shower. It's best when you don't plan it: If you look out the window at falling rain and wish you were out there—go!　　　　　　　—T. E.

- ❏ Follow my instincts
- ❏ Tell her how I really feel
- ❏ Call in sick to work and go roller-skating
- ❏ Surprise someone at least once a month
- ❏ Spontaneously fly to Paris for dinner
- ❏ Leave happy messages for people under their car windshield wipers
- ❏ Celebrate being single while I'm single
- ❏ Sit somewhere with a great view, a great friend, and a damn decent bottle of wine
- ❏ Spend a day away from my computer
- ✪ **Sleep on the beach**
- ❏ Allow myself to be wild, crazy, and irresponsible every once in a while

55

- [ ] Say, "Shut up and kiss me."
- [ ] Meditate for 5 minutes every morning
- [ ] Never take anything for granted
- [ ] Celebrate today

Plant rogue bulbs and wildflowers in unexpected places

Spread cheer in your community by choosing some of these low-maintenance flowers and planting them in abandoned lots or any patch of unclaimed green.

- Four weeks before the ground freezes in the fall, bury daffodil bulbs six inches deep, and cover them with dirt.

- Place tiger lily bulbs in partially shaded areas along tree or shrub lines, and cover the bulbs with four inches of dirt.

- Open areas with full sun, like abandoned city lots, are prime places for planting iris bulbs in the fall.

- Mexican star bulbs are perfect for areas with very dry conditions and poor or rocky soil.

- In early spring, put nasturtium seeds, along with a little soil, in abandoned pipes or between broken patches of sidewalk.

"I told a taxi driver to 'follow that bus!'"

I'd had a frantic day in town and was rushing to the bus stop to get home. The bus was just drawing away, and though the driver saw me, he continued going. A taxi was right by the bus stop and the driver had seen the whole thing. So I jumped in the taxi, shouting, "Follow that bus!" The taxi driver roared with laughter and said he'd waited twenty years to hear that. Off we went, threading and weaving through the traffic. Three stops down we caught the bus, the taxi stopping sideways across the road in front of it. Many passengers who had watched the "chase" were cheering and clapping—the taxi driver took a bow, but no fare, and I got a standing ovation when I got on the bus.

—G. W.

❏ Have one "pajama day" a month, refusing to get dressed and doing only what I want to do
❏ Take time to smell the roses
❏ Hitch a ride to work on a school bus
❏ Throw pebbles at my girlfriend's window
❏ Live my dreams instead of dreaming my life
❏ Spontaneously kiss a stranger

- ❏ Live life as a lark
- ❏ Make the most of the time I've been given
- ❏ Take a meandering walk with no destination
- ❏ Spend my days the way I want to spend my life
- ❏ Always buy lemonade when I see a kid's lemonade stand
- ❏ Remember that it is all temporary
- ✪ **Leave notes in library books**
- ❏ Let "yes" be my default answer
- ❏ Elope
- ❏ Go barefoot
- ❏ Always remember that tomorrow is not promised to me
- ❏ Live my life with arms wide open
- ❏ Follow my bliss
- ✪ **Think less and do more**
- ❏ Spontaneously break into song and dance
- ❏ Look at every morning as the beginning of a new adventure
- ❏ Stay hungry and stay foolish
- ❏ Take advantage of every opportunity
- ❏ Have a public pillow fight
- ❏ Howl at the moon

> ## "I went cloud gazing."
>
> I took a break from work and went outside to read my book in the beautiful spring sun. As I was lying there, the sky caught my eye and bewitched me for a good ten minutes. The clouds were moving fast in the wind and swirling as though trying to hypnotize. I hadn't experienced one of those "take my breath away" moments in a while. This was one of them.
>
> —S. T.

❏ Remember what it's like to be naive and innocent

❏ Live for today

❂ **Get kissed under the mistletoe**

❏ Give a flower to a stranger

❏ Race downhill on my bike and feel the wind in my hair

❏ Unexpectedly lick someone on the nose

❂ **Be more spontaneous**

❏ Take a moment each day to notice that I love my life

❏ Dance in the street

❏ Throw caution to the wind

❏ Wink at a stranger

❏ Stop planning and start doing

Write sonnets on bathroom walls

Class up your average stinky restroom with a little poetic graffiti. A fourteen-line sonnet is particularly well suited for a patch of bathroom wall and a whole lot nicer to read than your average "Jessie loves Steve" tag. Print out sonnets from Sonnets.org, keep them in your purse or pocket, and copy them onto public bathroom walls when the moment strikes you. Or avoid defacing public property and simply write out sonnets on cardstock and tape them to the walls or leave them on sink counters. It's a quick and easy way to pass on a bit of momentary pleasure to countless strangers.

❑ Spend the day in a hammock
❑ Bake a cake and eat it all myself
❑ Remember all important things last only a moment
✪ **Love life**
❑ Spend an entire paycheck on myself
❑ Sell my stuff and hit the road
❑ Live as if heaven is on Earth
❑ Whistle with a blade of grass
❑ Take a leap of faith
❑ Catch a leaf as it's falling from a tree

- ❑ Slow dance on a frozen pond
- ❑ See a concert on a whim
- ❑ Live my life unplanned
- ❑ Wake up on a beautiful morning, throw on my bathing suit, and lie in the sun
- ❑ Throw a public water balloon fight
- ❑ Anonymously leave fresh flowers on coworkers' desks
- ❑ Surprise my partner with a candlelight dinner
- ❑ Turn off my cell phone and don't check e-mail for an entire weekend
- ❑ Give people spontaneous high-fives

7

"Every parting is a form of death, as every reunion is a type of heaven." —*Tryon Edwards, theologian*

Reconnect
with Loved Ones

The history of your life can be charted by the people who were most important to you. Honor those connections by making a list of folks you've lost touch with over time and distance, and make it a goal to revive and nurture your relationships. Or find ways to rediscover what you love about those closest to you whose presence you've begun to take for granted. Repairing or reinforcing relationships can often be awkward, especially if it involves admitting you were wrong or reaching out to someone after several years of silence—but it's worth it. Make amends and let go of lingering tensions, get to know distant relatives and learn more about your roots, restore old friendships, and make a bridge from your past to your present.

- ☐ Form a mother/daughter group
- ☐ Reconnect with "the one that got away"
- ☐ Buy cheesy Valentine's Day cards and send them to all my single friends
- ✪ **Go home**
- ☐ Plan my birthday to be somewhere exotic this year and invite my close friends
- ☐ Try to fix the rift in my family
- ☐ Schedule a regular girls' night out
- ☐ Visit my long-lost family members in Greece
- ☐ Put people before work
- ☐ Have an Iron Chef competition with friends
- ✪ **Spend more time with Mom and Dad**
- ☐ Make a point of keeping in touch with people I've met on my travels
- ☐ Visit a neighbor once a week
- ☐ Organize a family reunion
- ☐ See my brother come home safely from Iraq
- ✪ **Stay in touch with my cousins**
- ☐ Start a poker night
- ☐ Take my daughter to a concert no matter how much I hate the music
- ☐ Reconcile with my sister
- ☐ Call my friends just to see how they are

○ **Go fishing with my dad**

❏ Apologize to my exes
❏ Develop a family website to keep in touch
❏ Spend more time with my kids
❏ Celebrate the people who supported me during difficult times
❏ Organize a high school reunion

Apologize

Saying you're sorry is rarely easy. It involves overcoming pride and hurt feelings and sometimes deciding that the relationship in jeopardy is more important than winning a disagreement. Sometimes it's easier to extend an olive branch by writing a heartfelt letter or sending a bouquet of flowers with a note. But nothing beats an apology made in person. It may mean giving the other person a chance to say their piece and air grievances, but don't get defensive—remember, your goal is to move on. If you don't think you can make a sincere apology, then you're not ready to apologize (people, especially when they're angry, can smell insincerity a mile away). But when it's done honestly and with feeling, looking someone directly in the eye and saying "I'm sorry" can be a powerful healer.

- ❏ Reconnect with my mentors
- ❏ Organize a happy hour with former coworkers
- ❏ Let go of old hurts and resentment toward family members
- ✪ **Make homemade pizza for friends every Friday night**
- ❏ Go on a cruise with my cousins
- ❏ Organize a siblings-only camping trip
- ❏ Meet my biological grandmother
- ❏ Find the courage to visit my mom's grave
- ❏ Meet my nephew
- ❏ Track down my first best friend
- ❏ Get to know my brothers better
- ❏ Find my mother

"I went on a date with my husband."

We went to dinner and were going to go to a movie. While at dinner, we were having so much fun just talking to each other that we decided to skip the movie and go to a bar to play a couple of games of pool. I can't wait to go out again.

—Y.L.W.

Start a family e-letter

If you have a big family it can be pretty hard to stay in touch with each and every one of them. A digital newsletter is a fun way to connect, or reconnect, with relatives you don't see often and keeps you updated on everyone's lives. Ask your grandparents or cousins to submit photos and write short paragraphs with their latest news. Choose a name for your newsletter, come up with deadlines for submitting information, determine a method and frequency of distribution, and pull together an e-mail mailing list. Newsletter templates are available with Microsoft Office, or you can create a digital version at FamilyPost.com.

❑ Host a Passover seder at my house for friends and family
❑ Go sailing with Dad
❑ Travel to Europe with a group of friends
❑ Reconnect with my college roommates
❑ Spend the day doing only what my son wants to do
❑ Look through old photo albums with my mom
❑ Visit my grandparents more often
✪ **Meet my online friends**
❑ Tell an old friend how sorry I am for what I did

- ❏ Host a "slumber party" party
- ❏ Call my dad just to say "hi"
- ❏ Have a spa day with my mom and sister
- ❏ Host Christmas for my family
- ❏ Reconnect with my wife
- ❏ Get to know my friends better
- ❏ Send my friends and family Christmas cards
- ⊙ **Go to my high school reunion**
- ❏ Send family members our wedding video
- ❏ Have guests for Shabbat at least once a month
- ❏ Make a list of all the friends and relatives I've lost touch with
- ❏ Invite my friends to a '60s party at my place
- ❏ Take my mom out for a fun day
- ❏ Rebuild my abandoned social life
- ❏ Reconnect with my high school sweetheart
- ❏ Compile a current list of all birthdays and special anniversaries
- ⊙ **Keep in touch with people who are important to me**
- ❏ Honor the choices my family members make
- ❏ Send postcards to my mother
- ❏ Call my grandmothers once a week

"I told my stepson that I love him."

My stepson has lived with me for the past three years, and I've always found it hard to tell him that I love him. I don't know if it's because I'm not his real dad or if it's simply because my parents were never very good at saying it when I was growing up. Either way, I want to start telling him. So last night when he was going to bed, I told him good night and that I love him. He responded with "See you later, alligator." It seems like such a small step, but it was scary to me. Hopefully now it'll be much easier.

—A. R.

❏ Meet family members in Ireland
✪ **Apologize to the people I've hurt**
❏ Keep in touch with my daughter
❏ Be available to friends and family, regardless of my mood
❏ Update my social network profiles
❏ Invite friends to afternoon high tea
❏ Keep in touch with my Army buddies
❏ Send birthday cards to all my friends
❏ Find the courage to look for my father

- [ ] Host a "Turning 35" party for old friends
- [ ] Organize a father-son tennis tournament this summer
- [ ] Drive across North America with my mother and get to know each other again
- [ ] Start a chain letter with my childhood friends
- [ ] Organize regular video-chats with relatives who are far away
- [ ] Make a list of people I've lost touch with and contact one person a month
- [ ] Don't be afraid to get back in touch

Get a lifetime e-mail address

Despite job changes and relocations, having an e-mail account that never expires means people will always know where to find you. Many schools offer lifetime e-mail addresses to graduates through alumni relations programs. A few e-mail providers offer lifetime forwarding such as PoBox (www.pobox.com). Once you acquire a lifetime e-mail account, send the new e-mail address to your entire contact list and ask recipients to use it as your permanent e-mail address. As your e-mail addresses change over the years, people will always be able to reach you.

"I talk to my parents more."

Parents can feel like a stifling influence, despite their best intentions, so sometimes the best thing is to get away. It was for me, anyway, first to college, then abroad, and now in another city. I think my relationship with my mom and dad has improved tremendously. Dad's a private sort of guy and he doesn't share personal thoughts and feelings very freely. So I had the bright idea to just write him a letter, updating him on my new life here in St. Louis, and wow, what a reply. A man of depth and warmth that's hard to see if you'd just met him—and a pretty decent writer to boot. It's like meeting someone brand new, and I intend on getting to know him even better. Ah, when parents become just . . . people.   —Z. G.

8

"A good cook works by the fire of imagination, not merely by the fire in the stove."

—*Robert P. Tristram Coffin, poet*

Cook More

Tantalizing aromas rising from steaming pots, the satisfying sound of vegetables sizzling in the skillet, and the creation of delectable dishes from a few basic ingredients are what make cooking one of life's great pleasures. It doesn't matter if your repertoire is limited to instant oatmeal—cooking is something anyone can, and everyone should, do. Central to every culture, food brings people together, provides comfort in times of sadness, and is the staple around which all celebrations center. Challenge your culinary skills and your taste buds by adopting goals to experiment with different cuisines, practice and perfect a signature recipe, or enroll in a cooking class. You'll learn that cooking not only nourishes the body but feeds the soul.

❏ Roast a duck
❏ Learn how to cook Mexican food
❏ Make baked Alaska
⚙ **Make yogurt**
❏ Start cooking at home again
❏ Cook over a campfire
❏ Take a class in culinary knife skills
❏ Bake vegan Twinkies
❏ Create a signature dish
❏ Cook with a new ingredient each week
❏ Grill pineapple
❏ Host a potluck every two weeks
⚙ **Make soup from scratch**
❏ Bake a giant cookie
❏ Fry an egg on the sidewalk
❏ Make my own jam
❏ Cook more vegan food
❏ Prepare a flambé
❏ Figure out how to smoke a turkey
❏ Host a Sunday brunch
❏ Deep-fry a pickle
❏ Have a barbecue in the middle of a snowstorm
❏ Make gnocchi from scratch
❏ Teach my daughter to whisk eggs

> ## "I love to host dinner parties."
>
> Dinner parties allow me to express my creativity in so many ways! I love planning the meal, searching for candles and tablecloths to liven up my house, the cathartic process of vegetable chopping, smelling the fragrance of garlic and onions. Most of all, it's the gathering together of friends of all interests and backgrounds and savoring the conversation and merriment that follows. —C. M.

❑ Invent a new type of cheese
❑ Make carob brownies
❑ Grill doughnuts for dessert
❑ Catch my own dinner
❑ Make egg rolls
❑ Cook with my kids
❑ Learn to cook fine Southern soul food
❑ Create my own spaghetti sauce recipe
❑ Don't be afraid to ignore the cookbook
❑ Limber up my stirring arm and make risotto
✪ **Learn to cook Chinese food**
❑ Crystallize creme brulée at the table with a blowtorch
❑ Compete in a national barbecue cook-off
❑ Invent a new cereal

Make sushi

Sushi lovers know that the only downside of this popular Japanese treat is the price. So why not skip the restaurant and make sushi at home? Many grocery stores now sell nori (thin, dried sheets of seaweed), short-grain white rice, and sashimi quality fish that has been frozen to kill bacteria. If you're worried about handling raw fish at home, you might start with recipes using vegetables or cooked seafood as the main ingredients, such as California or spider rolls. Before you begin making sushi, purchase a bamboo mat to mold rolls and consult recipes and step-by-step instructions at MakeMySushi.com. For one-stop shopping, consider *The Sushi Deluxe Book & Kit* by Kumfoo Wong.

✪ Bake my own bread
❑ Learn to cook without a recipe
❑ Get my father to teach me how to cook everything he knows
❑ Cook food that soothes the soul
❑ Go to the farmers' market every week and make a meal from what's fresh
❑ Perfect the art of Cajun cuisine
❑ Roast my own coffee

❑ Find a good vegetarian cookbook

❑ Cook a Thanksgiving dinner, *not* on Thanksgiving

❑ Create, enter, and have a recipe accepted as a finalist in the Pillsbury Bake-Off

❑ Grill trout over an open fire in Montana

❑ Cook with only organic foods

✪ **Make my own granola**

❑ Bake and decorate my best friend's wedding cake

❑ Have a fondue and wine picnic

❑ Create my own pizza

"I sit down to dinner with my family every night."

Every night it's a routine—"IT'S READY!" Then everyone piles in, sits down, and digs in. I like to hear the commotion, and if I get one "Yes, chicken!" or "Yum, tacos!" I call the meal a success! I have to admit there are some nights I wonder why I put myself through it—when everyone at the table seems to be having a bad day and is picking on the sibling to the right or left. But it's always interesting to see what the topic of conversation will be! I know that when my kids are grown and gone, I'm gonna miss saying, "IT'S READY!" every night!　　　　　　　　　　—B. U.

- ❏ Master the perfect French omelet
- ❏ Make a five-course dinner
- ❏ Host a neighborhood barbecue
- ✪ **Cook Thanksgiving dinner for my family**
- ❏ Make samosas from scratch
- ❏ Cook with herbs I grow myself
- ✪ **Invent a new ice cream flavor**
- ❏ Make a gingerbread house
- ❏ Enjoy a lobster fest on a Maine beach
- ❏ Make my mom's enchiladas
- ❏ Learn how to make homemade pasta
- ✪ **Make biscuits like Grandma did**
- ❏ Cook a romantic meal
- ❏ Learn how to prepare 20 healthy meals
- ❏ Dig for clams and then make clam chowder
- ❏ Perfect three delicious soup recipes
- ❏ Make an Oreo cookie milk shake
- ❏ Cook a rack of lamb
- ❏ Invent a salad dressing
- ❏ Preserve my own fruits and vegetables
- ❏ Prepare meals only from what's in season
- ❏ Create the perfect sandwich and name it after myself

Learn to Cook in Italy

Mouthwatering gnocchi, pasta topped with fresh, tangy tomatoes and tart olives, tender veal scallopini—such soul-pleasing dishes are quintessentially Italian. But cooking Italian food means more than following recipes or learning tricks of the trade from expert chefs. For a true lesson, you need to go to the source. In Italy, you'll learn the first rule of good cooking: Start with the freshest, best ingredients and do as little as possible to them. Take a culinary vacation offered by the International Kitchen (theinternationalkitchen.com) and you'll do more than just cook. You'll visit local produce markets, bakeries, vineyards, and olive presses, and will discover how the heritage and wine shape a particular region's cuisine. Take that knowledge back to your own kitchen and you'll never look at a bowl of pasta the same way again.

❑ Make pretty cupcakes
❑ Collect my family's recipes
❑ Cook breakfast on Saturday mornings
❑ Make an authentic Pad Thai
✪ **Cook for myself**
❑ Steam mussels

✪ **Make a soufflé**
☐ Learn to cook osso buco
☐ Create my own chili recipe
☐ Crystallize violets for cake decorations
☐ Make a pineapple upside-down cake
☐ Learn how to cook regional recipes of my homeland
☐ Learn how to make the perfect curry from scratch
☐ Cook a Tofurky

"I made chocolates."

I'm an admitted chocoholic—especially when it comes to the good stuff. And I adore truffles. I've always wanted to learn how to make them myself, and today I got the chance. I met up with my friend at her mom's place and spent hours talking, laughing, and making three different flavors of absolutely orgasmic balls of chocolate bliss: milk chocolate, Kahlúa, and rum. It was like some sort of exquisite grown-up mud play to get chocolaty up to my elbows while lovingly rolling each one by hand. And the taste . . . oh—pure heaven. I have a sweet pleasurebuzz throughout my whole body.   —R. D.

Enter a roadkill cook-off

Show off your cooking prowess by transforming groundhog, opossum, squirrel, or snake into gourmet cuisine at the annual Roadkill Cook-off in Marlinton, West Virginia (www.pccoc.com). Created more than a decade ago after West Virginia legalized the consumption of animals slain by moving vehicles, the cook-off has featured dishes such as "Smear the Deer Fajitas" and "Tire Tread Turtle Soup." (This is not as disgusting as it sounds. The whole point is to make these unlikely dishes as yummy as possible—not give you food poisoning.) Other roadkill cook-offs are held around the country, but if you can't find one locally, organize your own!

❑ Create my own recipe for organic sweet potato pie
❑ Make cheese using homemade vegetable rennet
❑ Make fudge
❑ Eat a different sandwich every weekday
❑ Learn better ways to use spices
❑ Buy new cookware
✪ **Make my own hummus**
❑ Cook Sunday dinner and eat in the dining room

9

"Independence is happiness."

—*Susan B. Anthony*

Be **Independent**

If a technical glitch wipes out your bank account, can your checkbook record provide a paper trail? If an unsavory character approaches you in a dark alley, can you protect yourself? If the stove catches fire, do you know how to use (and where to find) the fire extinguisher? If your best friend moves across the country or your significant other moves on to greener pastures, will you be able to pick up the pieces? Being independent is more than living on your own and paying the bills on time. It's about learning to rely on yourself in ways large and small, taking charge rather than accepting what's available, and finding ways to enjoy your own company. Think of *independence* as another word for inner strength and find ways to show that you are your own best protector, cheerleader, and friend.

- ❑ Spend at least one day a week by myself doing what I want to do
- ❑ Be the man and not work for "The Man"
- ❑ Care less about what others think
- ❑ Learn the difference between being alone and being independent
- ❑ Take more responsibility for myself
- ✪ **Confront my father**
- ❑ March to the beat of my own drum
- ❑ Confront my fears
- ❑ Think critically
- ❑ Get divorced
- ❑ Solve my problems on my own
- ❑ Stop borrowing money from my parents

"I took a self-defense class."

I took a self-defense class that was offered at the local YWCA. It was full contact, very informative, and adrenaline charged. (The scary thing was, about 75 percent of the ladies in the class had been attacked in one way or another.) But I feel stronger because now I know how to defend myself. This is very much worth it. It doesn't take much time, and it may save your life.　　　—F. F.

Go on a date with yourself

Sure, it may be awkward at first, but going to places alone is the ultimate test of your independence. If you can confidently walk into a restaurant and say to the maître d' "dinner for one," you've officially proved that you can be your own charming companion. Going places alone gives you a chance to soak up your surroundings and the space to reflect. So plan a solo trip to a museum or to the movies, or sit and have a drink at a sidewalk café and toast yourself for being such a confident individual.

❑ Make my living from music independent of the recording industry
❑ Save money for my own apartment
❑ Make a decision on my own without asking for advice
✪ **Move out of my parents' house**
❑ Stop relying on others for happiness
❑ Support myself
❑ Cook for myself
❑ Get rid of my cell phone and my e-mail and move to the mountains
❑ Make it on my own

Get a well-stocked tool kit

Your dad's not around to hang that shelf and the plumber wants a fortune to unclog your drain—it's time to do the job yourself. Having a well-stocked tool kit is the first step for any DIY maven. It should include the basics: a hammer and box of small nails, a measuring tape, Phillips and flat-head screwdrivers, adjustable socket and open-ended wrenches, and needle-nose pliers for gripping small objects. Two other useful tools are a vise grip for loosening stubborn screws or nails and a level with a built-in laser for installing shelves and hanging pictures. And Readers Digest's *New Fix-It-Yourself Manual* will teach you how to use them.

- ❏ Be independent in my relationships instead of codependent
- ✪ **Learn from my mistakes**
- ❏ Don't be afraid to sleep on my own
- ❏ Rely on myself
- ❏ Take charge of my life
- ❏ Rely less on technology
- ❏ Get up, dust myself off, and climb back on the saddle each time I get knocked down
- ❏ Learn to do my own taxes

- ❏ Defend myself
- ❏ Own land
- ❏ Go on a trip by myself
- ❏ Admit that my current romantic entanglement is stifling both of us, and summon the courage and love to end it
- ❏ Say no
- ❏ Live at my own pace
- ✪ **Remember that my choices are what create my reality**
- ❏ Remember that the world does not revolve around me
- ❏ Be brave enough to try things on my own

"I can change a flat tire."

It's easy, and I think it can be very foxy, not to mention helpful when you're in the middle of the desert and AAA is more than a couple of hours away. I've had to change four flat tires on the side of a road since I started driving six years ago. I have done it a couple of times in a pencil skirt and heels, and yes, I take pride in that. I think being able to change a flat is a sign of a strong, independent, hot woman.

—A.V.A.

- ❑ Learn and maintain healthy boundaries
- ❑ Start saving to buy a house
- ❑ Learn to fly and then get a plane so I can go wherever I want
- ❑ Live on my own terms
- ✪ **Own a house**
- ❑ Learn how to program my DVD player
- ❑ Don't lose myself in my next relationship
- ❑ Pay off all my debts
- ❑ Stand up for what I believe in, even if it's not popular
- ❑ Leave town and don't tell anybody
- ❑ Be a lifelong bachelor (or bachelorette)
- ❑ Take a solo trip to Europe
- ❑ Don't pay attention to fashion magazines

"I live on my own."

I've lived alone in my very own apartment for about five years. I still come home and relish the fact that I answer to no one, that the house is how I left it, that it is clean when I want it to be and dirty when I don't care. I am alone when I want and visited when I choose. I would not give up living in my own place for anything.   —I.V.Y.

Do your own laundry

Sometimes mastering the simplest of tasks is the quickest way to prove that you can take care of yourself. Here's what you need to know beyond "wash, rinse, and spin":

- Use an earth-friendly product like Ecover Stain Remover and pretreat any spots or smudges on clothes before tossing them into the hamper.
- Place lingerie or clothes made from acetate, acrylic, or rayon in a mesh laundry bag, and wash them on the delicate cycle with a gentle detergent such as Woolite.
- Preserve colors by turning pieces inside out, washing them in cold water, and hang drying them.
- Add a cup of baking soda to the rinse cycle to soften your wardrobe, remove odors, and brighten clothes.
- Fold clothes immediately after removing them from the dryer to ward off wrinkles.

❑ Spend a weekend doing things on my own
❑ Don't be afraid to do something my parents might not approve of
❑ Quit my job and start my own business

10

"Staying focused takes less talking and more thinking. It requires no procrastination and all determination."

—*T.C.P., 43 Things member*

Stay Focused

When it comes to the art of staying focused and getting things done, there's no single strategy that works for everyone. Some people need to be tied to their desk in a soundless chamber, others need the freedom to roam and make their own schedule. Whatever your method for dealing with a big project (or a list of goals), focus (not trolling the Web for celebrity gossip) is the fuel that will propel you forward. Some of your goals may be small tasks, others big dreams. But whether you want to finally put together that family scrapbook or start your own business, clearly defining your goals, setting deadlines, and developing techniques to boost your concentration are vital to your success. As legendary Hollywood producer Samuel Goldwyn said, "The harder I work, the luckier I get."

❑ Pursue my dreams until they become a reality
❑ Get up when the alarm goes off
❑ Give 100 percent
❑ Be more determined
❑ Resist the temptation to settle
❑ Complete my most hated task every day
❑ Set life goals to keep me motivated
❑ Be more efficient when working
✪ **Spend less time online**
❑ Create a 5-year plan
❑ Take life step-by-step
❑ Prioritize and follow through
✪ **Avoid postponing tasks until tomorrow**
❑ Keep my mind, eyes, and heart focused
❑ Don't waste time on self doubt

"I try to accomplish one thing each evening."

I start by getting up every time a commercial comes on and doing part of a task. Sometimes I stop and go back to the TV, but a lot of times I find myself wanting to finish my task and I forget to go back to the TV!   —R. A.

Reward yourself in little ways

Rewarding yourself with a little gift or mini celebration after completing a task is a great way to keep yourself motivated. Create a list of incentives—a dinner out, soaking in a hot bath, a special bottle of wine—and reward yourself after each milestone.

❑ Maintain a daily schedule rather than a to-do list

❑ Always do my job (whether I like it or not)

✪ **Admit what I really want**

❑ Don't waste my precious time

❑ Improve my project management skills

❑ Improve my work ethic

❑ Focus on school

❑ Live for myself and no one else

❑ Be more disciplined

✪ **Don't give up**

❑ Don't let my long to-do list overwhelm me

❑ Draw a roadmap for where I want my life to go

❑ Create an online task manager

❑ Don't allow myself to be persuaded by people who have their own ulterior motives

❑ Concentrate more on short-term goals

Improve your concentration

Increasing your concentration requires staying alert, hydrated, and able to manage distractions. Use these five tips to boost your productivity.

1. Drink at least eight glasses of water a day and avoid sugary or caffeinated drinks that give you bursts of energy followed by an inevitable crash.

2. Snack on high-protein foods like peanut butter to fire up your brain. Avoid carbohydrates, which induce sluggishness.

3. Fight fatigue by taking a break every forty-five to ninety minutes. Go outdoors. Walk around, stretch your legs, or do arm circles to promote circulation and reduce tension.

4. Get plenty of rest. Sleeping fewer than eight hours a night diminishes your ability to concentrate.

5. Rather than stopping the work flow to turn to unrelated tasks (like confirming who's driving the carpool on Monday or finally ordering that new bookcase), write them down on a notepad as they occur to you and take care of them during a break or at the end of the day.

✪ **Do first things first**

❑ Work 4 uninterrupted hours each day

❑ Find a focusing mantra to repeat to myself whenever I get distracted

❑ Keep things in perspective

❑ Do one thing at a time

❑ Work on developing skills that will benefit my life

❑ Split my big goals into tiny easy-to-achieve tasks

✪ **Stay motivated**

❑ Set aside 30 minutes a day to reflect on my goals

❑ Reduce distractions

❑ Spend less time on Instant Messenger

❑ Push my limits

❑ Make it happen

❑ Work hard

❑ Spend less time planning and more time "doing"

❑ Be less apathetic

❑ Be completely ruthless about getting things done

❑ Stick with it even though it's not all "fun" because I want the results

✪ **Ask for help when I need it**

❑ Be shockingly productive

❑ Work ahead of deadlines

✪ **Be on time for work**

❑ Visualize success
❑ Take the first step toward my commercial venture
❑ Make the most of my 30s

Make S.M.A.R.T. goals

S.M.A.R.T is a strategy made popular by management consultant Peter Drucker to ensure that your goals are well defined and achievable. Each letter represents an important element of this strategy.

1. Avoid any ambiguity by making a goal *Specific* and clearly outlining its purpose and the desired results.
2. Find a way to *Measure* progress, such as checking off days on a calendar, noting details in a journal, or mapping out milestones.
3. Be sure the goal is *Attainable*: Can it be achieved with a reasonable amount of effort? Do you have the necessary skills and knowledge to complete the task?
4. Keep goals *Relevant* to your bigger life plan by defining the personal or professional benefits of accomplishing them.
5. Deadlines help. Establish a fixed schedule with a start and end point to make goals *Time*-bound.

> ## "I set realistic goals."
>
> I started out setting some pretty lofty and fanciful goals on 43 Things because they sounded fun to dream about. However, I'm finding that the smaller, more attainable goals are actually more fulfilling because I can do things, even just small things, to work toward them on a daily basis. Don't get me wrong, I'm still leaving some "dream-on" goals, like visiting the wreck of the *Titanic*, but realistic equals rewarding, even if it's just something like finishing a quilt. I may only get one billionth of the quilt done each night, but I can look at my progress and feel that I'm accomplishing something! —L. G.

❏ Cultivate self-discipline

❏ Set career goals

✪ **Don't become an old man who wishes he had done . . .**

❏ Remember what is important to me

❏ Get over my fear of failing by visualizing what it would feel like, accepting it, and moving on

11

"I can only think of music as
something inherent in every
human being—a birthright.
Music coordinates mind, body,
and spirit."

—*Yehudi Menuhin, violinist and conductor*

Make Music

Every musician has experienced it: that moment when you play the riff flawlessly, a friend applauds, a pretty girl in the audience smiles, and you think, "I could get used to this." For some, this moment becomes a lifetime pursuit of fame, but most musicians eventually learn that the song is its own reward. There's nothing wrong with rock star dreams, but the joy of music happens at karaoke parties, jam sessions with bandmates, or your child's first recital. Don't let playing wrong notes or singing off-key stifle your inner musician. Rescue your old band instrument from the closet, bust out that electric guitar, or just sing in the shower. Make each note matter, celebrate the spaces in between, and as the Detroit punk band MC5 urged us in the summer of '69, "Kick out the jams!"

✪ Find my one karaoke song

❑ Learn to play "Für Elise"
❑ Write a song
❑ Learn how to read music
❑ Open a recording studio
❑ Compose a mash-up
❑ Collect more music
❑ Rap
❑ Form an '80s cover band
❑ Sing in a jazz choir
❑ Join an orchestra
❑ Broadcast my music over the Internet
❑ Learn to play "Heart and Soul" on the piano
❑ Jam more often

✪ Be the lead singer in a band

❑ Learn to play a musical instrument
❑ Become a DJ
❑ Start a Beatles cover band
❑ Focus on my music again
❑ Learn to play the fiddle
❑ Sing soul music

✪ Conduct an orchestra

❑ Have a classical quartet with a rock-and-roll
  mentality

> ## "I play music with friends."
>
> I play regularly with a quartet, but we play only for
> our own enjoyment. It is the most wonderful way to
> make music: with a small group of friends, working
> on the repertoire and getting it to sound like we want;
> experimenting with different interpretations and discussing
> different ways of approaching the music.   —H. S.

❏ Be in a gospel choir

❏ Create my own techno music

❏ Sing the blues

❏ Listen to a new piece of classical music
  every day

❏ Find a place for my band to practice

✪ **Compose music**

❏ Sing in the youth choir

❏ Learn to play Mozart's 25th piano concerto

❏ Be in a punk band

✪ **Start a record label**

❏ Study with a great musician

❏ Play R&B saxophone

❏ Join a country rock band

❏ Buy a new album every week

- ❏ Play mandolin in a jazz band
- ❏ Sing in a barbershop quartet
- ❏ Become an expert in a style of music I know nothing about
- ❏ Be an opera singer
- ❏ Sing on top of a building in Chicago
- ✪ **Play a solo with a symphony orchestra**
- ❏ Sing a Billie Holiday song on stage in a blues club
- ❏ Reunite my band
- ❏ Play Beethoven's "Moonlight Sonata" on a grand piano

Sell your music

Record labels are dinosaurs. Releasing your music to the world has never been easier. Think niche marketing (begin with friends and family), and shoot for Internet fame over record sales (remember those round disc thingies?). Launch your band website for free with MySpace (www.myspace.com) or step up to Bandzoogle (www.bandzoogle.com). Sling MP3s via GarageBand (www.garageband.com) and CDs via CDBaby (www.cdbaby.com), along with Amazon's music store, iTunes, or eMusic. Log-in and rock out!

"I recorded my own song."

So, two nights ago, my cousin and I recorded a version of his song with me doing backup vocals. The next day, I was on this creative high. I felt so alive when we were recording, it was soul-moving. My cousin said something like, "I think you're more yourself when you sing than the rest of the time," and it struck a chord with me—because I think he might be right.   —P. E.

❏ DJ parties and weddings
❏ Record an album of traditional folk songs
✪ **Learn to play piano**
❏ Transform pots, pans, and wooden spoons into a drum set and play it with my kids
❏ Play in a polka band
❏ Learn to play the xylophone
❏ Sing in a pub
❏ Jam with Metallica
❏ Perform my songs at local venues
✪ **Get a record deal**
❏ Compose children's music
❏ Sight-read sheet music
❏ Start an ABBA cover band

❏ Play violin in an electric string quartet

✪ **Write and record an album**

❏ Sing with my kids in the car

❏ Make a song that becomes a Top 40 hit

❏ Practice my scales every day

❏ Compose a symphony

❏ Start a marching band

❏ Perform in a jazz festival

❏ Play the banjo at least once in public

❏ Go to a juke joint in Mississippi

❏ Be in a Christian rock band

❏ Learn to play the cello

✪ **Compete in a "Battle of the Bands"**

❏ Play blues saxophone under a bridge

❏ Sing R&B

❏ Perform in a local musical

❏ Do vocal percussion in an a cappella chorus

❏ Be in an all-girl glam rock cover band

❏ Sing in a cabaret

❏ Play the steel drums on my 50th birthday

❏ Form a New Wave metal band

❏ Hit the high notes

❏ Sing an entire song in Spanish

❏ Conduct Beethoven's Symphony No. 7

Enter a karaoke contest

Karaoke may have its roots in 1970s Japan, where dinner-party guests performed songs for entertainment, but today the popular amateur pastime is a way for talented vocalists to compete for prize money, trophies, and recognition at hundreds of contests around the world. So if your rendition of "Sweet Child o' Mine" brings down the house at the local karaoke night, then go for the big time and register for the Karaoke World Championships (www.kwc.fi). Contestants who wow judges in their home countries are rewarded with a trip to the finals and the opportunity to showcase their singing talent on the international stage.

❑ Perform "Fever" in a smoky jazz club
❑ Be a street performer
❑ Perform in a community orchestra
✪ **Teach music**
❑ Get into my school's jazz band
❑ Scat like Ella Fitzgerald
❑ Go to Spain and learn how to play
   flamenco guitar
❑ Learn to play the spoons
❑ Sing the *Messiah* with a choir

"I'm taking voice lessons."

I can't think of anything that makes me happier than the memory of standing next to the baby grand with my friends, our voice coach at the piano, singing "Tonight" from *West Side Story* and laughing hard at each other and ourselves if we tripped up. Taking voice lessons is like achieving something I only dreamed about when I was younger. I have no illusions of performing. I'm simply content to enjoy this experience before worrying about the "next step."   —J. M.

❏ Own a vintage guitar
❏ Enrich my children's lives with music
⊙ **Make a living playing my trumpet**
❏ Perform at the Edinburgh Fringe Festival
❏ Get a solo in my choir
❏ Play bebop guitar in a kickin' trio or quartet
❏ Play the tuba
❏ Build my vinyl collection
❏ Record a concept album
❏ Write a song for my lover
❏ Get my band out of the garage
❏ Play the organ at a baseball game
❏ Listen to all of my parents' old records

- ❏ Tour the world with my band
- ❏ Build a home recording studio
- ❏ Play the guitar with a violin band
- ❏ Write an opera
- ❏ Become a master with looping and tape effects
- ❏ Get discovered while playing on the streets of Nashville
- ❏ Build a one-man band contraption
- ✪ **Create the ultimate playlist**
- ❏ Record sounds in my neighborhood and loop them into a song
- ❏ Stop talking about learning an instrument and do it

12

"There are few things as beautiful and rewarding as being an improved version of the person that you were yesterday."

—B.J., 43 Things member

Be a **Better Person**

Becoming a better person isn't about perfection—it's about becoming the best version of you. It's fine to have role models— a friend with a kind heart, a passionate professor, or a caring neighbor—but don't fall victim to other people's standards. You might start by identifying the qualities you most value—loyalty, warmth, generosity—then take an honest look at your own strengths and weaknesses. Only you can define what constitutes progress. Think of it as a soulful kind of self-improvement— a correcting of faults and smoothing of rough edges. Keep your promises, practice forgiveness, and above all, remember humility—because you're never finished finding new ways to improve your lovely, imperfect self.

❑ Ask for help when I need it
❑ Improve my karma
❑ Be a loyal and loving partner
✪ **Practice compassion**
❑ Stand up for myself
❑ Find beauty in the small things
❑ Quit being so selfish
❑ Learn to tell a great story
❑ Be more self-aware
❑ Understand how my actions affect others
❑ Do what is right, not what is easy
❑ Use only what I need
✪ **Be less judgmental**

"I'm becoming a better listener."

My husband is often quiet and I realize that's one of the things I love about him—he really listens and doesn't always have to add his own two cents. I started modeling my behavior after his: making eye contact, nodding to show I'm listening, and not speaking too often. When I did speak, I'd often rephrase what the person was saying so that they knew I understood them. It took a lot of conscious effort, but now I listen better and I think others appreciate it. —G. B.C.

- ❏ Purge the word *jealousy* from my vocabulary
- ❏ Give 10 percent of my income to charity
- ❏ Make happiness a priority
- ❏ Be a leader, not a follower
- ✪ **Be a better friend**
- ❏ Make people laugh
- ❏ Show love to all living creatures
- ✪ **Communicate better**
- ❏ Volunteer in my community
- ❏ Be generous with my time and patience
- ❏ Learn humility
- ❏ Have a sense of humor
- ❏ Be helpful to others
- ❏ Learn to be an active listener
- ❏ Be more devoted to my faith
- ❏ Have more confidence
- ❏ Practice kindness
- ❏ Listen to my heart instead of my fears
- ❏ Be more open-minded
- ❏ Inspire others to act with wisdom
- ❏ Be more supportive of others
- ✪ **Live passionately**
- ❏ Learn to say no
- ❏ Say what I mean and mean what I say

- ❏ Be a more caring person
- ❏ Learn tactful honesty
- ❏ Keep in touch with old friends
- ❏ Show people I love them with actions, not just words
- ❏ Be more flexible—go with the flow
- ❏ Admit when I'm wrong
- ❏ Be more informed about current events
- ❏ Overcome my prejudices
- ✪ **Practice forgiveness**
- ❏ Don't make assumptions
- ❏ Live with an open heart
- ❏ Get to know my neighbors
- ✪ **Live with integrity**
- ❏ Support local businesses
- ❏ Be a warm host
- ❏ Have good manners
- ❏ Learn to express myself better
- ❏ Turn weaknesses into strengths
- ❏ Spend more time with my kids
- ❏ Strengthen my willpower
- ❏ Make more of each day
- ❏ Stop being so distant with my family
- ❏ Tell my kids I love them every day

Treat everyone as you wish to be treated

If you've ever worked retail, you know that people can be less then polite. It's easy to take for granted the folks we deal with over the course of the day. Your interactions may not last longer than a minute, but it is these small, common courtesies that help make the world a better place.

- Always make eye contact with sales clerks and service employees.
- Abstain from talking on your cell phone while conducting business transactions.
- Keep your cool and be gracious when dealing with customer service representatives, no matter how frustrating the circumstances. Remember, they don't make the rules.
- Talk to someone you see every day but don't know. If you don't have time for small talk, at least acknowledge them with a smile and kind greeting.

❑ Stop my wasteful spending
❑ Do something selfless every day
⚙ **Be better than I was yesterday**
❑ Make an effort to socialize more

"I practice patience with my wife."

Sometimes life is busy and stressful for both of us. I need to remind myself to be patient. It's not always easy. But, as I read somewhere once, "Love is patient and kind." Those words have always resonated with me.   —K. P.

- ❑ Be more efficient when working
- ❑ Work on my ability to compromise and negotiate
- ❑ Do a better job of recycling
- ❑ Help one person every day
- ❑ Give people the benefit of the doubt
- ❑ Keep my promises
- ✪ **Be more accepting of others**
- ❑ Don't jump to conclusions
- ❑ Be decisive and take charge of situations
- ❑ Always be prepared
- ❑ Help the environment
- ❑ Be better than average
- ❑ Grow from painful experiences
- ❑ Give at least one compliment every day
- ❑ Be spontaneous once in a while

❑ Always say "please" and "thank you"

❑ Stay positive in the face of adversity

❑ Get through a tough time without losing my mind

❑ Stop gossiping

❑ Don't be a slob

❑ Challenge my own prejudices

❑ Respect my elders

Be a better conversationalist

The art of conversation is as much about making people feel at ease as it is about witty repartee. Here are some things to remember:

- Maintain eye contact.

- Respect differing viewpoints, be careful not to squelch someone's enthusiasm about a topic, and use lighthearted comments to defuse potential disagreements.

- If someone begins monopolizing the discussion, direct the conversation back to the original person or topic.

- When a new person joins the group, widen the circle, introduce yourself during the next break in conversation, and engage him or her by asking a question.

❑ Become a better kisser
❑ Learn to accept failure and loss
⊙ **Lead a balanced life**
❑ Recognize my faults and accept them
❑ Provide love to those who need it most
❑ Don't slack off at my job
❑ Be more approachable
❑ Clean up after myself
❑ Get in touch with my femininity
❑ Play hard, work harder

Have better manners

Manners go beyond knowing which fork to use and sending thank-you notes. Manners are about showing respect for others. From saying no gracefully to telling noisy neighbors to quiet down, good manners help you finesse sticky situations with aplomb and avoid hurt feelings. To navigate all kinds of modern etiquette land mines, pick up *Miss Manners' Guide to Excruciatingly Correct Behavior* by Judith Martin or, of course, the inimitable Emily Post. Pass good manners on to less-than-perfect kids with Judi The Manners Lady's instructional CD from www.themannersclub.com.

"I am a mentor to my students."

For me, the key to being a good mentor is humility and excellent listening skills. You have to be unafraid to show your human side. I've been through a lot with my students. I've dealt with their school, family, work, and other personal issues. They come to me with everything, and frankly, I love it. I'm proud that they rely on me as a source of inspiration.

—S. H.

❑ Advocate for equality for all
✪ **Don't give up**
❑ Accomplish tasks as soon as I'm given them
❑ Be closer with my siblings
❑ Find beauty in small things

13

"The first wealth is health."

—*Ralph Waldo Emerson*

Be Healthy

Whether we run triathlons and snack on soybeans or use the treadmill as a drying rack, it always feels like we should be doing more to stay healthy. It's not surprising, considering the frequency with which another miracle cure, superfood, vitamin, or workout program emerges as the best new way to get fit and stay healthy. It can start to feel as overwhelming as, say, running twenty-six miles. Forget the fads and start small. Walk to the store instead of driving, drink one less cup of coffee a day, ditch the sweet dessert and enjoy some fresh fruit instead. Slowly add some bigger goals to your list, like exercising regularly or losing ten pounds, and remember that the real promise you're making is not to follow every healthy rule in the book, but to start treating your body with the respect it deserves.

- ❏ Try acupuncture
- ❏ Eat less junk food
- ✪ **Lose 10 pounds**
- ❏ Pack a healthy lunch for work
- ❏ Take an "X" out of my size
- ❏ Go to a health spa for a week
- ❏ Get more antioxidants
- ❏ Deadlift 500 pounds
- ❏ Break free of my carbohydrate addiction
- ✪ **Drink 8 glasses of water each day**
- ❏ Move toward an organic, natural lifestyle
- ❏ Go raw
- ❏ Eliminate fried foods and foods with high-fructose corn syrup
- ✪ **Go to sleep earlier**
- ❏ Increase my stamina
- ❏ Get my hearing tested
- ❏ Do at least 30 crunches a day
- ✪ **Exercise more**
- ❏ Skip dessert
- ❏ Come home from the grocery store with ONLY healthy food
- ❏ Go for a daily walk at lunchtime
- ❏ Get buff

> ## "I take a walk every day."
>
> I walk over a mile every day, sometimes much more. I wish
> I could walk everywhere. You can see so much more on foot,
> listen to music, and never have to worry about traffic. What I
> really love is how it provides a sense of scale. Cars (and worse,
> airplanes) cover distance so quickly, you really have no idea
> how big the world actually is. I love to feel small—it reminds
> me how important I am to the world (i.e., not very!).   —L. L.

❑ Lose 5 pounds each month till I reach my goal weight

✪ **Join a gym**

❑ Buy a treadmill

❑ Eat more tofu

❑ Get tested for celiac disease

❑ Keep a food diary

❑ Stop yo-yo dieting for good

❑ Get a complete blood test

❑ Do Pilates

❑ Get rid of the knots in my shoulders

❑ Cleanse, tone, and moisturize my face daily

✪ **Do 100 consecutive push-ups**

❑ Drink less soda

❑ Build a home gym

Shop the periphery of the supermarket

When you go grocery shopping, shop *only* around the periphery of the store—that's where all the fresh food is. Try to avoid the middle aisles where the processed food lives. Why are processed foods so bad for you? First, to give them a longer shelf life, processed foods are stripped of valuable nutrients, which is why they're said to contain "empty calories." Second, and worse, they often contain unhealthy trans fats, saturated fats, and large amounts of sugar and salt as well as food additives. If you stick to the edges where the fruit, vegetables, or dairy products live, you'll be less apt to want to put those unhealthy nonfoods into your body.

❑ Get more calcium

✪ **Eat only when I'm hungry**

❑ Go to the dentist

❑ Live to be 100

❑ Don't eat fast food or vending-machine food for two weeks

✪ **Get in the best shape of my life**

❑ Eat less dairy

❑ Do breathing exercises every day for a month

❑ Get a Pap smear

❑ Eliminate salt
❑ Wash my hands more often
❑ Beat my thyroid disease
✪ **Lift weights**
❑ Take better care of my mental health
❑ Switch from coffee to green tea
❑ Eat smaller portions
❑ Get my blood sugar under control
✪ **Practice yoga daily**
❑ Eat fewer TV dinners

"I read ingredient labels."

My son was having some behavioral problems, and I thought that instead of taking him to see a doctor, I'd try working with his diet first. And boy oh boy, am I glad I did. As soon as I removed foods with artificial dyes from his diet, there was an AMAZING improvement. He's still an active, happy little guy, but now he has the self-control that he was lacking—and he is able to get to sleep at night. And now that we're in the habit of checking labels, I look for other things, too. We're eating healthier all the way around. (And my son is even getting in the habit of label reading—a skill that will be very good for him into the future.)   —H. W.

- ❏ Ride my bike every day
- ❏ Have my mercury levels tested
- ❏ Take a step class
- ❏ Work out in the morning
- ❏ Get a facial
- ❏ Set up a yoga/exercise space in my home
- ❏ Get a personal trainer
- ✪ **Consume less sugar**
- ❏ Join Weight Watchers
- ❏ Eat an apple a day
- ❏ Stick with my low-carb diet
- ❏ Walk a marathon
- ❏ Be able to do pull-ups
- ❏ Reduce the amount of meat in my diet
- ❏ Lower my cholesterol
- ✪ **Run more**
- ❏ Get an HIV test
- ❏ Control my diabetes through diet
- ❏ Get a massage
- ❏ Get an allergy test
- ❏ Practice martial arts
- ❏ Drink wheatgrass juice
- ✪ **Gain weight**
- ❏ Use olive oil when I cook

Detox your body

Multiple cups of coffee, burgers and fries for lunch, your evening wind-down cocktail—it's time to give your poor system a break! It doesn't have to be forever and it doesn't have to be all at once, but cutting out some of the foods and drinks that are less than great for you is like giving your body a mini tune-up. The goal shouldn't necessarily be to lose weight, but to make you more conscious of what you're putting in your body and how it's making you feel. Check out Kathy Freston's twenty-one-day cleanse in her book *Quantum Wellness* or read *The 4-Week Ultimate Body Detox Plan* by Michelle Schoffro Cook.

❏ Beat cancer
✪ **Tone my body**
❏ Never eat at fast food restaurants again
❏ Wear sunscreen every day
❏ Survive menopause
❏ Eat more fish
✪ **Run a mile without stopping**
❏ Have more energy
❏ Do a colon cleanse
❏ Get checked for skin cancer

"I stopped eating junk food."

My skin has cleared up, I don't feel lethargic or sluggish anymore, I can fit into smaller jeans, and I've found that healthy food tastes so much nicer and makes you feel good while you're eating it! Apart from ice cream in the summer and chocolate at "that time of the month," I don't eat junk food anymore. I don't even crave it. —A. B.

- ❑ Eat more salad
- ❑ Run 10 miles a week
- ✪ **Quit smoking**
- ❑ Don't eat anything that contains ingredients I can't pronounce
- ❑ Get on birth control
- ❑ Give up caffeine
- ❑ Stay sober
- ❑ Buy a new toothbrush
- ❑ Get an eye exam
- ❑ Bicycle 200 miles in a month
- ❑ Have a flat stomach
- ❑ Eat fewer processed foods
- ❑ Work out my arms
- ❑ Ride the stationary bike every day

✪ **Be a vegetarian**
❑ Eat more broccoli
❑ Complete my chemo treatments
❑ Stop emotional eating
❑ Floss more
❑ Use my home workout videos more often
❑ Get my iron levels tested
❑ Eat more vegetables
❑ Walk 2 miles at least 5 days each week
❑ Use natural remedies to improve my mental health

✪ **Have better posture**
❑ Go on the Atkins diet
❑ Run until I feel the sweat drip down my back
❑ Get a mammogram
❑ Run a 10K
❑ Take vitamins daily
❑ Collect information on my family's
medical history

✪ **Drink less alcohol**
❑ Reverse my osteoporosis through weight-bearing
exercise
❑ Take time to relax every day
❑ Beat Hodgkin's lymphoma
❑ Get an annual check-up

Stretch every day

Stretching increases your flexibility, improves your posture, and relieves tension. It also feels really good. Here are a couple of easy ones you can do in front of the TV.

- Lie on your back. Bring your knees up to a ninety-degree angle. Keeping your shoulders on the ground, allow both knees to fall slowly to the right. Extend your left arm, turn your cheek to the left, and gaze out over your fingertips. Hold for sixty seconds and repeat on the other side.

- Standing with your feet slightly wider than shoulder-width apart, bend at the waist and try to touch the ground. Hold for sixty seconds. Still bent over, turn your upper body toward your right leg and hold for sixty seconds, then turn toward your left leg and hold.

- Bring your shoulders up to your ears and roll them back and down and then forward in slow, continuous circles. Reverse the direction. Repeat five times each way.

- Using a wall for support, bend your right knee, bringing your heel to your buttock, and grab your ankle with your right hand. Hold for sixty seconds and give your quadriceps a good stretch. Repeat with your left knee.

❑ Kick my sugar habit for good

❑ Eat more fiber

❑ Eliminate trans fats from my diet

✪ **Lower my blood pressure**

❑ Start doing Yogilates

❑ Give up aspartame

❑ Take a nutrition class

❑ Cut MSG out of my diet completely

✪ **Be more flexible**

❑ Find a good doctor

❑ Try new healthy recipes with my family

❑ Give myself monthly breast exams

❑ Get rid of my migraines

14

"Our perfect companions never have fewer than four feet." —*Colette*

Get a Pet

Dogs have the reputation of being man's best friend, but the same could be said for parrots, ferrets, or fish. Whether they have fur, feathers, or fins, our animal pals provide us with companionship and love. It's not surprising that research shows that pet owners have lower blood pressure and are less prone to depression. But as anyone who has impulsively brought home a kitten from the local shelter will tell you, there's more to having a pet than filling the food and water dishes, giggling at adorable antics, and getting wet kisses. The sleepless nights, mysterious smells, emergency trips to the veterinarian, and furniture or clothing casualties will certainly test your patience. Once the annoyance fades, however, you'll find that you're as devoted to them as they are to you.

- ❏ Train my cat to walk on a leash
- ❏ Foster an injured animal
- ❏ Own a wiener dog
- ❏ Spend more time with my pet
- ❏ Teach my bird new tricks
- ✪ **Own a horse**
- ❏ Give my cat more toys than any other cat on the block
- ❏ Get a parrot
- ❏ Take my dog to a dog spa
- ❏ Get a rabbit
- ❏ Have an awesome aquarium
- ✪ **Train a hunting dog**
- ❏ Own a hairless cat
- ❏ Build a gym for my kitty
- ❏ Spay my cat
- ❏ Do agility training with my dog
- ❏ Get a Labradoodle
- ✪ **Own a lizard**
- ❏ Accept that my cat hates me
- ❏ Run with my dog
- ❏ Build a cat tree for my cat
- ❏ Get a chinchilla
- ❏ Install a doggie door

- ❑ Get a snake
- ❑ Own a Scottie dog
- ❑ Have my cat vaccinated
- ❑ Make spending time with our pets part of my "transition from work to home"
- ❑ Get my own potbellied pig
- ❑ Have a Siamese cat
- ❑ Brush my dog more often
- ✪ **Adopt a cat**
- ❑ Milk a cow
- ❑ Become a member of PETA

"I have ferrets."

Make sure you get two! They love having a buddy. I have Puck and Grendel. They are freakin' darling. They are always ready to play, use their litter box religiously, sleep in a furry heap on their hammock, and beg for treats. They walk on leashes and are super with the little kids in my neighborhood. If you clean the litter box, supplement their water, and spray their living space with a pet-safe deodorizer, you'll hardly notice any musky smell. Just make sure you have enough time to play with them: They are hyperactive!

—S. L.

- ☐ Teach my dog to play with a Frisbee
- ☐ Have a dog named Cat and a cat named Dog
- ☐ Get a turtle
- ☐ Take my dog to obedience training
- ✪ **Pet my dog more**
- ☐ Teach my parrot to talk
- ☐ Befriend a squirrel in my backyard
- ☐ Improve my relationship with my cat
- ☐ Own an exotic animal
- ☐ Feed my pet only organic food
- ☐ Teach my pet some manners
- ☐ Come home with a box of puppies

"I foster kittens."

I've managed to foster a few kittens when space is at a premium at the local cat shelter. It's a good deal for everyone. I keep them for a few weeks while they learn how to be held—and how to claw furniture and steal food off my plate. When space at the pet shop (which works with the shelter) opens up, they get a highly visible cage—and soon after, a nice family. While it's not always easy to give them back, I'm happy to help in some small way by giving them a nice childhood.   —T. L.

Adopt an animal

More than six million cats and dogs enter animal shelters each year and only about half are adopted—the rest are put down. So why buy an expensive purebred when there are countless playful friends looking for a loving home? Go to www.petfinder.com, which profiles pets from more than ten thousand shelters in North America, and find your new best friend!

❑ Adopt a retired racehorse
❑ Walk my dog by the ocean
❑ Own a duck
❑ Play fetch with my cat
❑ Brush my dog's teeth once a week
❑ Open an alpaca farm
❑ Go to the dog park more often
❑ Work with animals
❑ Build cat walkways in my house
❑ Get a guinea pig (and get him a friend)
❑ Breed my mare
❑ Install a cat door
❑ Teach my dog to heel
❑ Clean the litter box once a day

- ❏ Buy a llama
- ❏ Build a bigger and better rabbit cage
- ❏ Decide what kind of pet to get
- ❏ Get a hamster
- ❏ Train my parakeet to whistle
- ⊙ **Own a monkey**
- ❏ Get a scrappy little dog and name him Speck
- ❏ Have a pug and basset mix
- ❏ House-train my dog
- ❏ Take my dog swimming
- ❏ Adopt a retired greyhound
- ❏ Learn about different breeds of dog
- ❏ Get my new puppy to sleep through the night

"I volunteered at an animal shelter."

I helped people find their lost pets, I watched an old couple bring in their elderly dog to be put down because it was too old to walk, a little boy cry over losing his dog because they weren't allowed to keep it in their apartment, people giving up their pet because they were being deported. The emotional aspect of it—odd as it sounds—made me appreciate things in my life a lot more.   —R. V.

Teach your cat to do tricks

It's not true that cats are lazy and can't be trained. They can learn to sit, walk on a leash, stay, lie down, and can even be potty trained. Here's how to teach your kitty to shake hands.

1. Before each meal put a treat in your hand and let your cat smell it.
2. Cup the hand that doesn't have the treat and hold it out.
3. When the cat puts a paw into the cupped hand, say, "Good kitty!" or some other type of praise.
4. Reward the cat with the treat.

Learn how to teach your cat other tricks by visiting www.catsplay.com or www.bestfriendspetcare.com.

15

"Most people are about as happy as they make up their minds to be."

—*Abraham Lincoln*

Be Happy

Happiness can take on many forms—feeling the
wind in your hair, enjoying a picnic with friends,
letting go of old anxieties, forgiving a wrong—
and with it comes a lightening of spirit and
an opening of the heart and mind. Happiness
begets happiness—the more you cultivate, the
more you experience. But how do you find it in
the first place? Besides vowing to laugh more
and smile for no reason, 43 Things members
have discovered that relishing life's simpler
pleasures and countering disappointments with
positive thoughts are key tools in the quest for
happiness. So count your blessings, always
be on the lookout for new sources of delight,
choose to perceive happiness where you might
not have before, and write your own happy
ending.

- ❑ List all the things I did well today
- ☼ **Surround myself with beauty**
- ❑ Run on the beach for the sheer joy of it
- ❑ Refuse to let the past affect my future
- ❑ Celebrate arcane holidays
- ❑ Be cheerful in any situation
- ❑ List 43 things I like about myself
- ❑ Remember the good times
- ❑ Surround myself with laughter
- ❑ Think big thoughts but relish small pleasures
- ❑ Keep negative people out of my life
- ❑ Drink champagne and giggle
- ❑ Find reasons to do the Happy Dance
- ❑ Work fewer hours, leaving time for more important things
- ☼ **Accentuate the positive, deemphasize the negative**
- ❑ Find satisfaction in the stuff I get done instead of fretting over stuff that's still pending
- ❑ Laugh at what makes me angry
- ❑ Indulge in guilty pleasures
- ❑ Respond to a critical thought with five positive ones
- ❑ Feel pleasure or joy at least once every day

"I smile more."

It gets positive results! People hold doors open for me, shopkeepers will take time to wrap gifts nicely and chat (sometimes throwing in freebies!), colleagues will help when I ask with a warm smile—even if it's an unpleasant task. If the day has gotten off to a bad start, then I smile at someone and a chain begins—smiling makes the world a sweeter place!

—R. C.

❑ Try my best, and be happy with what I achieve

❑ Document kindness, selfless acts, beautiful moments, and gentle amusements

✪ **Be happy in my own skin**

❑ Watch 21 funny, funny movies

❑ Have one whole week in which I feel happy

✪ **Daydream**

❑ Enjoy my weekends

❑ Share laughter with at least one person every day

❑ Do things that make me a better person, rather than things that just make me feel better

❑ Smile until I feel it

❑ Enjoy the sunshine

❑ Have no regrets

Practice the Happiness Manifesto

This set of guidelines for attaining bliss was derived from a 2005 research study by Dr. Richard Stevens and a team of experts involving residents of a London suburb. Cultivate a happy life by practicing these ten steps.

1. Plant something and nurture it.
2. Count at least five blessings at the end of each day.
3. Take time to talk—have an hour-long conversation with a loved one each week.
4. Phone an old friend and arrange to meet up.
5. Give yourself a treat every day and take the time to really enjoy it.
6. Have a good laugh at least once a day.
7. Get physical—exercise for half an hour three times a week.
8. Say hi or smile at a stranger once each day.
9. Cut your TV viewing by half.
10. Spread some kindness—do something nice for someone every day.

✪ Laugh my way through life
❑ Celebrate the mundane
❑ Live happily ever after

- ❏ Be more optimistic
- ❏ Begin and end my day with positive affirmations
- ❏ Be happy without being in love
- ❏ Find at least one thing each day that makes me happy
- ❏ Enjoy the silence
- ❏ Rediscover 10 simple pleasures
- ❏ Cry because I'm so happy
- ❏ Jump for joy
- ❏ Listen to music that makes me happy
- ❏ Be enthusiastic in the face of indifference
- ❏ Make time to relax
- ⊙ **Make a difference in someone's life**
- ❏ Celebrate things that are never celebrated
- ❏ Live for today and don't worry about tomorrow
- ❏ Go through a day without being negative
- ❏ Celebrate our anniversary every month
- ❏ Make exercising more fun
- ⊙ **Be happy with what I have**
- ❏ Write down one thing to look forward to in my future each day
- ❏ Never give up seeing good in the world
- ❏ Experience true joy
- ❏ Be happy being single

- ❏ Run or work out to release endorphins
- ❏ Laugh with my kids
- ❏ Appreciate my family
- ❏ Smile even when I'm sad
- ❏ Indulge in something I would NEVER, EVER do
- ✪ **Don't hold grudges**
- ❏ Do things that make me laugh just for the sake of it
- ❏ Be OK with doing nothing
- ❏ Have some mindless fun
- ❏ Remember that I am loved
- ❏ Find balance between life and work
- ❏ Pamper myself once a week
- ❏ Think happy thoughts
- ❏ Jump up and click my heels together
- ❏ Be happy for no reason
- ❏ Practice hopefulness
- ✪ **Smile every day**
- ❏ Don't let other people's negativity affect me
- ❏ Giggle uncontrollably
- ❏ Have a party to celebrate me
- ❏ Be selfless
- ❏ Be able to laugh at myself

> ## "I stopped caring about what other people think."
>
> One day I realized that when other people liked themselves—really, truly liked who they were—then I did, too. After that, I simply concentrated on becoming the kind of person I could confidently say I liked. It worked. It doesn't matter to me what others think because I like who I am and will continue to do so whether or not I have others' approval.
>
> —A. B.

❏ Make a list of things that make me smile, giggle, or laugh out loud and invite others to add to it!

◌ **Learn to take criticism**

❏ Figure out why I get so depressed sometimes

❏ Write down 100 happy thoughts to remind me of how good things are [see Chapter 43]

◌ **Don't take life too seriously**

❏ Celebrate another day of living

❏ Be less sarcastic

❏ Celebrate victories—great and small

❏ Have fun at work

❏ Surround myself with people who love me for me

◌ **Wake up happy**

- ☐ Overcome my sadness
- ☐ Be happy—not on-the-surface happy, but deep-down-for-serious happy
- ✪ **Celebrate imperfection**
- ☐ Laugh every day
- ☐ Don't be bitter
- ☐ Enjoy the inane and celebrate the nonsensical

Reframe an unhappy ending

In his book *Happier,* based on his popular course at Harvard, Tal Ben-Shahar, Ph.D., argues that happiness can be learned. One of the many exercises he recommends is to take a negative experience and recast it in a positive light.

Write about a difficult time—a failure, a loss—describing it in as much detail as possible. Then, without minimizing the pain, think about the lessons it may have taught you. Are you more resilient? Smarter? Less afraid? Now list the good things you've taken away from the experience. You can do this on your own, but consider doing it with a small group of trusted friends who may see positive results that you can't see yourself. In doing this exercise, you'll learn that perception is everything, and by changing the way you see something, you can change the way you feel about it.

> ## "I write down the things that make me happy each day."
>
> Today, yesterday, and the day before it was:
>
> - a Sunday evening drive through the rain with splashy sounds and bright reflections in windowpane drops.
> - a walk around the lake. There was so much life everywhere—things growing, swimming, running around. It was beautiful, even if the sun was feeling shy.
> - a positively decadent bath with candles and a delicious bath bomb. Afterward, my body was hot and relaxed, and my hair was whirly and wild. —R. U.

❑ Figure out how not to be depressed without chemicals

❑ Be happy and kind to myself every day

✪ **Count my blessings**

❑ Celebrate my creativity

❑ Don't let idiots get me down

❑ Accept compliments

❑ Forgive those who are hardest to forgive

✪ **Be kind**

❑ Forget the bad times

- ❏ Focus on positive things in my life
- ❏ Live each day filled with hope and purpose

✪ Be needed

- ❏ Spend more time laughing with my best friends
- ❏ Be more carefree
- ❏ Do something for myself
- ❏ Don't let other people's negativity affect me
- ❏ Make myself look pretty every day— dress to be happy

✪ Celebrate life

- ❏ Define what happiness means to me
- ❏ Cultivate my five senses
- ❏ Appreciate the little pleasures I get in my job
- ❏ Focus on long-term goals of happiness instead of short-term pleasures

✪ Stop and smell the roses

- ❏ Feel fully alive
- ❏ Give hugs every day
- ❏ Find happiness by spreading happiness
- ❏ Find a story with a happy ending and read it when I feel down

Compile a "songs that make me happy" playlist

Summon good thoughts, get karma flowing in a positive direction, and pump yourself up with a kick-ass mix guaranteed to improve your mood. Stumped about what to include? Here are some happy-making song suggestions:

- "Walking on Sunshine" by Katrina and the Waves
- "Beautiful Day" by U2
- "I've Got the World on a String" by Frank Sinatra
- "Good Day Sunshine" by The Beatles
- "What a Wonderful World" by Louis Armstrong
- "I Got You (I Feel Good)" by James Brown

16

"Choose a job you love, and you will never have to work a day in your life." —*Confucius*

Love My Job

Spend a few minutes pondering this little
factoid: On average, half of the waking hours
of your adult life will be devoted to punching
the time clock. Does that make you want to
jump for joy or jump off the nearest bridge?
If it's the latter, it's time to dust off the résumé
and chart your next move—away from that job
and maybe that career. (The cost of staying put
will be measured in your happiness, so don't let
financial fears trap you.) If you're lucky enough
to enjoy your work, draft a plan to make sure
you don't lose that loving feeling—because
dream jobs that aren't nurtured can grow dull.
Remember: The best job may not be high profile
or high paying; it just has to be something that
is meaningful to *you*.

- ❑ Get a promotion
- ⚙ **Get a better-paying job**
- ❑ Get a job with a company that appreciates honesty and hard work
- ❑ Come home from work exhausted but fulfilled
- ❑ Escape a life of corporate servitude
- ❑ Do at least two things every week to advance my candidacy for my dream job
- ❑ Find what it is that would make me happy professionally
- ❑ Support myself through art
- ❑ Ask for an evaluation from my boss
- ❑ Send out one résumé a day

"I work from home."

I didn't think I'd ever be able to motivate myself enough to work from home and actually get work done, but I surprised myself. I've discovered that I'm much more productive on days when I sleep until I'm ready to wake up (no more alarm clock!), take time to eat breakfast, and spend time with my dog. Since I'm not working hourly for a paycheck, I just work until what needs to be done is done.

—S. S.

Have a killer résumé

Think you've got a great résumé? Reread it and check
that you've done the following:

- List achievements rather than responsibilities.
- Proofread for spelling and grammatical errors
  (and then do it again).
- Use action verbs when describing accomplishments
  (*developed, contributed, implemented*).
- Tailor the information to the position you're applying for.
- Try to fit everything on a single page.

Check out Résumé Resource (www.resume-resource.com)
or Monster.com (www.career-advice.monster.com/resume-
writing-basics/) for advice, templates, critiques, and content
guidelines.

❏ Find my dream job
❏ Get a challenging job
✪ **Become a spy**
❏ Find work that inspires me and plays to my
strengths
❏ Figure out what career track I'm looking for
❏ Do more things that will look good on my résumé
❏ Get an excellent review at work

Learn to network

Networking is the key to unearthing new career opportunities. You never know when a friendly conversation will result in an informational interview, a job offer, or business deal. So consider these tips to expand your contact list and meet new faces:

- Attend lectures focused on your industry to learn about developing trends and new technologies while connecting with others in the field.
- Enroll in short university courses directed at your peers or those in upper management and build your résumé while getting to know colleagues.
- Participate in the local chapter of your alumni association. That quiet guy from your Western Civ class, the hot girl who lived in your freshman dorm, that obnoxious R.A. —all those kids are now adults with jobs and connections to be mined.
- Connect with current and former business associates using networking websites like LinkedIn (www.linkedin.com), where you digitize your Rolodex and expand your contacts beyond your current network.

❑ Own a farm
❑ Promote my blog
❑ Work with kids
✪ **Get paid to travel**
❑ Get a job where I'm respected for what I do
❑ Open a teahouse
❑ Find a mentor
❑ Work four days a week
❑ Find a flexible job
❑ Make a good living from creative pursuits
✪ **Update my résumé**
❑ Promote myself
❑ Get a job that I can be proud of
❑ Own a coffee shop
❑ Earn the respect of my colleagues
❑ Get my own office
❑ Go to networking events
❑ Get a job I am worthy of
❑ Join a women's networking group
❑ Find the courage to quit my current job
✪ **Get paid to write**
❑ Find new ways to promote my business
❑ Work abroad
❑ Escape my cubicle

- ❏ Work in an environment that allows me to be silly and unpredictable
- ✪ **Become a journalist**
- ❏ Love my job every day
- ❏ Be more appreciated at work
- ❏ Find a job that doesn't conflict with my moral convictions
- ❏ Be the editor-in-chief of a radical and influential art and fashion magazine
- ❏ Be my own boss
- ❏ Work from home
- ❏ Ask friends to review my résumé

"I found a job that I love."

I hated my job. I was good at what I did, but it had really started to change me—I was becoming cranky, angry, and cynical. SO . . . I quit. I got a student loan and went back to school for something I had always wanted to do. I wanted to be a hairstylist. I was always told there was no money in that job (wrong), that it was not satisfying work (wrong), that it was grueling (wrong). The moral of the story? Work is such a big part of your life. If you're not happy, it's time to rethink your career.   —C. S.

Ask for a raise

Approaching the boss about a pay increase can be a nerve-racking experience, but not if you get in the right mind-set. Realize that the worst-case scenario isn't your superior saying no, it's the company losing an irreplaceable employee—you. To prepare for salary negotiations:

- Schedule an appointment to talk about your future at the company (in other words, don't take your boss by surprise).
- Quantify your achievements to calculate your worth.
- Demonstrate a passion for your job, talk about planned projects and goals, and outline how your skills will benefit the organization in the future.
- Choose a minimum salary increase and don't accept less without significant perks (have a list of these handy).

❏ Find a new career in a new town
❏ Make my hobby my profession
✪ **Find work I'm passionate about**
❏ Find a job where I can use the skills I learned from my college major
❏ Work in a creative field

- ❑ Get paid for helping people
- ❑ Get out of the rat race
- ❑ Make a lot of money while I'm young and retire early
- ❑ Create a business plan for starting my own company
- ❑ Bartend on the weekends
- ❑ Create my own website to showcase my writing and art
- ✪ **Quit my day job**
- ❑ Tell my boss how I really feel
- ❑ Love my job because it fulfills me, not because it pays me
- ❑ Have my own cooking show
- ❑ Be an Internet celebrity
- ❑ Change careers at age 45
- ❑ Figure out "what I want to be when I grow up"
- ❑ Go into business with my family
- ❑ Have a career, instead of just a job
- ❑ Don't make my work my life
- ❑ Work outdoors
- ❑ Find a job that pays enough money so that I can finally buy a house
- ❑ Refuse to do busy work ever again

"I quit my job."

I quit my job two weeks ago. I felt like I was stifled, strangled, and smothered. There is a point at which we remember who we are and how we want to show up in the world. People are dying every day. Some of them die in jobs that no longer serve them. Some die living their dreams. Since each day is a gift, I have chosen to look for something that will be more fulfilling for me. I left with bills and some debt, but I am happy every day knowing that, until I decide differently, this is my time to live boldly.   — L.D.G.

❏ Find one good thing about my job every day
❏ Do what I love and trust that the money will follow

17

"Bad habits are like chains that are too light to feel until they are too heavy to carry." —*Warren Buffett*

Stop It

Bad habits have a tendency to stick around so long they become second nature. Over the years, quirky behavioral tics seem to multiply and we start making excuses, such as "I was born this way" or "That's just how I am." Nail biters become smokers, a series of fibs snowballs into pathological lying, and the wild weekends of your youth turn into a serious drinking habit. Suddenly, the little voice rooted in the part of you that knows better is yelling "STOP IT!" You're not alone. Goals such as "stop procrastinating" and "stop caring what other people think of me" are fixtures on the life lists of 43 Things' members—along with promises to battle more dangerous behavior, from ending affairs to gambling to stealing. So, what devilish habits do you want to defeat?

- ❏ Stop comparing myself to other people
- ❏ Stop starting my sentences with the word "I"
- ❏ Stop hitting the snooze button
- ❏ Stop picking my nose
- ❏ Stop being so bossy
- ❏ Stop criticizing the bad things in others that I see in myself
- ❏ Stop having an affair
- ❏ Stop losing my wallet
- ✪ **Stop being lazy**
- ❏ Stop settling
- ❏ Stop being codependent
- ❏ Stop wondering "What if . . ."
- ❏ Stop mumbling
- ✪ **Stop being so angry**
- ❏ Stop frowning
- ❏ Stop slouching
- ❏ Stop having nightmares
- ❏ Stop being so neurotic
- ❏ Stop being such a follower
- ✪ **Stop overanalyzing**
- ❏ Stop nagging
- ❏ Stop stuttering
- ❏ Stop daydreaming

"I stopped drinking alcohol."

Alcohol can be good at appropriate times and in appropriate amounts. Unfortunately for some people—like me—it can consume them. Stopping is not easy, because it requires an admission of weakness, something few people will do voluntarily in private and almost never in public. Yet, once I admitted a lack of power to control my drinking and sought help, the rest was fairly easy. I don't lie or make excuses. I just say I don't drink. End of story. —G. T.

✪ **Stop being paranoid**
❑ Stop slacking
❑ Stop fighting
✪ **Stop being selfish**
❑ Stop drifting
❑ Stop being a victim
❑ Stop being so naive
❑ Stop being narcissistic
❑ Stop sabotaging myself
❑ Stop cutting myself
❑ Stop stealing music
❑ Stop being so moody
❑ Stop lying to myself

Stop being late

It may feel like there aren't enough hours in the day, but the reality is that being punctual is an important part of time management and can help you reclaim some lost hours. Stop being late with the following tips:

- Don't overschedule yourself. Politely explain to coworkers, children, or friends that you can't take on additional commitments.
- Be realistic about how much time something is going to take. If you have a meeting across town, add in extra time for traffic, finding parking, getting to the meeting spot, and anything unexpected.
- Wear a watch and synchronize every clock in the house, the office, and the car. Then arrive everywhere ten minutes early.
- Plan ahead. Take a few minutes at the end of each day to review the following day's schedule. Then finish up any small loose ends so you aren't constantly playing catch-up.

❏ Stop being mean
❏ Stop being so anxious
✪ **Stop complaining**

- ❑ Stop being messy
- ❑ Stop being a cliché
- ❑ Stop partying
- ❑ Stop being so dramatic
- ❑ Stop smoking weed
- ❑ Stop being an enabler
- ❑ Stop being greedy
- ✪ **Stop gossiping**
- ❑ Stop being a martyr
- ❑ Stop being superstitious
- ❑ Stop being ashamed
- ❑ Stop chewing the inside of my mouth
- ❑ Stop overindulging
- ❑ Stop stereotyping
- ❑ Stop being hypocritical

"I stopped watching TV."

My husband and I turned off our cable service in 2002. It is absolutely worth it! We read more books, talk more, eat dinner together, and are less susceptible to advertising. We do watch the occasional movie or TV show on DVD, but all in all we spend less than three hours a week in front of our television. I don't miss it one bit! —S. P.

- ❏ Stop being rude
- ✪ **Stop binge eating**
- ❏ Stop being pretentious
- ❏ Stop underestimating myself
- ❏ Stop wanting what I don't have
- ❏ Stop apologizing for myself
- ❏ Stop being fickle
- ❏ Stop being wasteful
- ✪ **Stop being so judgmental**
- ❏ Stop doing things I don't believe in
- ❏ Stop panicking
- ❏ Stop being so down on myself
- ❏ Stop wishing I were younger
- ❏ Stop being claustrophobic
- ❏ Stop jaywalking
- ❏ Stop womanizing
- ❏ Stop being spoiled
- ❏ Stop weighing myself
- ✪ **Stop hating myself**
- ❏ Stop spending more than I have
- ❏ Stop being a ditz
- ❏ Stop blaming myself
- ❏ Stop craving attention in public
- ❏ Stop being so rebellious

Stop wasting time on the Internet

In many ways the Internet has been a boon to productivity, but it can also be a major time suck. Use the following tips to keep your time spent online in check:

- Use MeeTimer to record and analyze where you spend your time online. (In other words, those two hours and thirty-nine minutes you spent chatting with friends via Instant Messenger just ate up 6.5 percent of your work week.) Download this add-on at www.mozilla.com/firefox/.
- Decide to spend only five to ten minutes surfing the Net before getting back to work (or life), and then set a timer to keep you honest.
- At home, turn off the computer when you've finished online tasks to break the habit of constantly checking e-mail, browsing news, or shopping.
- Turn off e-mail notification features and check and respond to messages only at specific times.

❑ Stop calling in sick when I'm hungover
❑ Stop Googling myself
✪ **Stop blushing**
❑ Stop being afraid of success

"I stopped buying things I don't need."

There comes a time when you have no space left in your apartment, no money, no credit, and that's when I figured out it was time to stop shopping compulsively. I joined Debtors Anonymous (www.debtorsanonymous.org) and followed their suggestion to write down every cent I spend, make, or have given to me. I have cut up and canceled my credit cards. When I go shopping, I make a list and buy only what I need. Learn the difference between need and want, be honest with yourself, and save your money for something really worthwhile.   —S. C.

- ❏ Stop sleepwalking
- ❏ Stop breaking promises
- ❏ Stop being ordinary
- ❏ Stop being afraid
- ✪ **Stop obsessing**
- ❏ Stop thinking about her
- ❏ Stop buying lattes
- ❏ Stop listening to other people
- ❏ Stop working so hard for so little
- ❏ Stop being clumsy and breaking everything

❏ Stop being afraid of commitment

✪ **Stop overreacting**

❏ Stop playing video games

❏ Stop interrupting

❏ Stop freaking out about turning 30

❏ Stop cracking my knuckles

❏ Stop being afraid of making a mistake

❏ Stop getting into fights

❏ Stop looking for love

❏ Stop shopping with my credit card

❏ Stop turning into my parents

❏ Stop being a hypochondriac

❏ Stop running from my problems

✪ **Stop being depressed**

❏ Stop being so serious

❏ Stop flirting

❏ Stop getting parking tickets

✪ **Stop being a perfectionist**

❏ Stop getting library fines

❏ Stop being so sarcastic

❏ Stop snacking

❏ Stop hurrying

❏ Stop pretending

✪ **Stop gambling**

- ❏ Stop bragging
- ❏ Stop reading too much into things
- ❏ Stop being a workaholic
- ❏ Stop being so promiscuous
- ❏ Stop getting my hopes up
- ❏ Stop taking caffeine pills
- ❏ Stop being so sensitive
- ✪ **Stop staying up so late**
- ❏ Stop reading daily horoscopes thinking they will change my life
- ❏ Stop being afraid of death
- ❏ Stop having crushes
- ❏ Stop being dependent
- ✪ **Stop crying**
- ❏ Stop working through lunch
- ❏ Stop being so predictable
- ❏ Stop being so competitive
- ❏ Stop getting annoyed so easily
- ❏ Stop taking cabs
- ❏ Stop dwelling on the past
- ❏ Stop getting distracted
- ✪ **Stop doubting myself**
- ❏ Stop arguing
- ❏ Stop whining

Stop biting your nails

Nail biting is a common stress-reliever, but it's also an unsightly dirty habit that can cause nail, mouth, and gum infections and contribute to dental problems. Use the following tips to help you stop:

- Give yourself regular manicures and put clear or colored polish on your nails.
- Coat nails with bitter-tasting polish such as Control-It (www.controlitcream.com).
- Wear gloves or cover your nails with stickers or tape to remind yourself not to gnaw on them.
- Whenever you start biting your nails, take a break, switch activities, or breathe deeply to reduce stress.

☐ Stop doing things for money that destroy my soul
✪ **Stop loving him**
☐ Stop following celebrity gossip
☐ Stop stealing
☐ Stop picking at my skin
☐ Stop blaming myself
☐ Stop running from relationships

18

"People are born for different tasks, but in order to survive everyone requires the same nourishment: inner peace."

—*Sri Sathya Sai Baba, spiritual leader*

Find **Inner Peace**

There are moments when everything just feels right. Your mind is still, your body relaxed, your spirit fed, and you find, if only for a moment, peace. These moments are hard to plan; they usually just well up in you. It could be an evening spent gazing at the twinkling city lights from a hilltop, hearing your favorite song played live, or taking a walk on a crisp fall day. You may not be able to bottle the feeling, but you can cultivate it. Internal turmoil isn't always avoidable, but there are ways to widen your reserves of inner strength, still the tremors of anxiety, and let go of regret and fear. Whether you listen to your heartbeat or listen to the sound of waves crashing on a beach, quiet your mind, find balance, and engender a sense of wholeness that will radiate outward.

- ❏ Retreat from the chaos of my life
- ✪ **Create a Zen garden**
- ❏ Practice yoga
- ❏ Find a balance between the things I want to do and the things I need to do
- ❏ Worry less
- ✪ **Try acupuncture**
- ❏ Let go of the past
- ❏ Balance my chakras
- ❏ Have quiet time each day
- ❏ Take a spa vacation
- ❏ Visit an ashram
- ❏ Make time for myself
- ❏ Quiet this constant sense of urgency
- ❏ Spend a year in a Buddhist monastery
- ❏ Breathe deeply
- ❏ Control my temper
- ❏ Forgive and forget
- ❏ Make a place in the garden for contemplation
- ✪ **Don't take things so personally**
- ❏ Go on a yoga retreat
- ❏ Sit in a tree and watch the world go by
- ❏ Cultivate peace
- ❏ Create my own mental oasis

❑ Look for the positive and appreciate it
❑ See the beauty in every person
❑ Overcome depression
❑ Find clarity of thought
❑ Take a hot bath by candlelight
❑ Have a day of complete relaxation
✪ **Make peace with my family**
❑ Spend a weekend doing absolutely nothing
❑ Get hydrotherapy
❑ Tend bonsai trees
❑ Practice meditation
❑ Love without fear
✪ **Don't sweat the small stuff**
❑ Get a massage
❑ Accept my weaknesses
❑ Get over my ex

"I listen to my heartbeat."

If you can learn to listen to your heartbeat in the middle
of your forehead, then you will be able to clear your mind.
Simply focusing on that heartbeat brings you to your center.
And that is where you find you are. When you do this, you
are experiencing the now. For the now is all we have. —D. F.

Go on a silent retreat

iPod buds shoved in our ears, noisy traffic outside our bedroom windows, TV blaring every night—sometimes it's hard to hear yourself think! Escaping from all that noise (along with daily stress and distractions) into a world of silence can be a powerful way to nourish inner peace. Here are some places to quiet down:

- Silence reigns at the Spirit Rock Meditation Center in California. Talking is permitted only during daily dharma discussions and one-on-one talks with instructors. (www.spiritrock.org)

- Founded in Kentucky in 1848, the Roman Catholic Abbey of Gethsemani invites the public to stay at the abbey and join the monks in their program of daily prayer rituals, silent reflection, and sacraments. (www.monks.org)

- In the Berkshire Mountains of Massachusetts is the Kripalu Center for Yoga and Health, with retreats that combine yoga, meditation, courses in Buddhist thought, and outdoor activities. Meals can be silent, and quiet hours are observed each day in the evening and early morning. (www.kripalu.org)

- ❑ Value time spent alone for introspection
- ❑ Quiet my mind
- ❑ Find a very dark place to look at the stars in silent solitude

✪ **Have more patience**
- ❑ Spend more time on the beach with sand between my toes
- ❑ Join a Zen meditation group
- ❑ Memorize poems that relax me

✪ **Accept aging**
- ❑ Find enlightenment in my lifetime
- ❑ Come to terms with death
- ❑ Accept imperfection
- ❑ Listen to my inner voice
- ❑ Get restful, uninterrupted sleep every night

✪ **Be present in the moment**
- ❑ Reach a state of absolute bliss
- ❑ Be less nervous
- ❑ Accept the world for what it is
- ❑ Practice mindfulness
- ❑ Find the good in all situations
- ❑ Relax in a hot spring
- ❑ Overcome my anxiety
- ❑ Find a mantra

"I forgave my mother."

It took me a long time, but about a year ago I finally let go and realized that my mom is just another human being fumbling her way through the world—just like me. Once I fully accepted this, my perspective changed and my anger toward the world diminished considerably. I'm a much more relaxed person these days, and I find that it's becoming easier for me to accept and forgive my own faults and mistakes. Forgiving your parents is not easy, but it's a very worthwhile endeavor.　　　　　　　　　—T.S.M.

- ❏ Make my home a sanctuary
- ❏ Get over my first love
- ❏ Enjoy the silence
- ❏ Accept that I can't do everything
- ❏ Buy a cabin in the mountains
- ✪ **Cry**
- ❏ Care less about material possessions
- ❏ Feel completely free
- ❏ Lighten up and take life less seriously
- ❏ Practice tai chi
- ❏ Trust myself
- ❏ Live alone in the woods for a month

❏ Have my energy rebalanced by a holistic healer
❏ Smile more
❏ Soak in a Jacuzzi
✪ **Avoid drama**
❏ Find a way to express myself
❏ Live in harmony
❏ Conquer chaos
❏ Take weekends off

Breathe deeply

Deep, calming breaths reduce tension and settle an overactive mind or spirit. But breathing deeply (and properly) requires a little practice. Here are a few simple tips for mindful breathing:

■ Breathe from your diaphragm. Place a hand on your abdomen and feel your belly gradually swell as you inhale and then contract as you exhale.

■ Slowly lengthen each inhale and exhale. Start by using a count of three to inhale and a count of three to exhale. Then extend that to four, and then five counts or longer.

■ With each breath do a mental scan of your body: Relax your jaw, shoulders, head, hips, legs, and any other areas where you might be holding tension.

✪ Pamper myself
❑ Resolve conflicts
❑ Lounge in a hammock

✪ Be more Zen
❑ Ignore what others think of me
❑ Lie in a meadow, forget everything and
 feel the sun on my skin
❑ Practice stillness
❑ Live by the sea

✪ Let go
❑ Have no shame
❑ Stop obsessing about the things I can't change
❑ Sit by the lake and watch the sunlight on
 the water

"I have quiet time every day."

Make a commitment to observe a daily quiet time. It's awesome to save some special time for yourself, to think about your life, feel the world, watch the beauty of nature, and feel at peace. Read affirmations, inspiring quotes, or poetry. Close your eyes and visualize a favorite vacation spot. Listen to your favorite music. Take a short walk. Practice a relaxation technique or breathing exercises. Have some tea.   —D. C.

Keep a journal

Keeping a journal is a simple yet powerful way to engage in self-reflection. Some things to keep in mind:

- Reserve time each day or week when you're not likely to be interrupted, like before bedtime or Sunday mornings.

- Turn off the TV, ask not to be disturbed, and spend a few minutes focusing on your breath and quieting your mind.

- Let your subconscious roam and jot down whatever comes to mind. Don't think too hard about what you put on paper, and don't censor yourself. Leaving out details in order to paint a rosier picture will only serve to confuse what should be a clarifying process.

- Don't reread what you wrote—at least not right away. These private musings should be safe from judgment and criticism.

❑ Love myself
✪ **Simplify my lifestyle**
❑ Sit back and enjoy the view
❑ Live without regrets
❑ Sit quietly and enjoy my own company

19

"Life is partly what we make it,
and partly what it is made by the
friends we choose." —*Tennessee Williams*

Have More Friends

Your friends are the people who console you after a bad day or breakup, celebrate your successes without a whiff of envy, and step in with encouraging words when things don't go your way. They're the ones who make you laugh 'til you cry, finish your sentences, and can be counted on to drive the getaway car. No matter how intelligent and independent you are, life will throw you curveballs and you need a team to rally around you. Having close friends means there is always someone to listen to your problems, help you plan your comebacks, hear your darkest secrets, and keep you honest. Cultivating best friends as well as a cadre of casual ones means you'll always have good company, supportive hugs, and shoulders to cry on.

- ❏ Meet a couple of fabulous people who become lifelong friends
- ❏ Be my daughter's friend
- ❏ Be less judgmental of people I don't know very well
- ❏ Find the balance between talking too much and talking too little
- ❏ Start a backgammon club
- ❏ Figure out how to be a friend
- ❏ Join an outdoor adventure group

✪ Don't be lonely

- ❏ Start a study group
- ❏ Have friends who understand me
- ❏ Throw a party
- ❏ Turn acquaintances into friendships

✪ Have a best friend

- ❏ Make a friend in every country
- ❏ Be more confident
- ❏ Make new friends and forget old enemies
- ❏ Create a meaningful social life
- ❏ Introduce myself to more people
- ❏ Find people with different interests to open me up to new experiences
- ❏ Join a walking group

"I stopped being shy."

I was terribly shy and socially awkward. One day, I got fed up and decided that social interaction was like anything else and that if I practiced, I would get better at it. I started writing down a goal for myself every day. Day one was to talk to a stranger. Once I'd written it and had it stare me in the face, I felt like I had to do it. Every day, I tried to push myself a little further—more people, longer conversations. The first several times were difficult and awkward, but the more I did it, the easier it got, and the easier it got, the more confident I became. I've practiced to the point that it's coming naturally to me. Looking back now, it seems so silly to be afraid of people. I feel like I wasted years of my life being shy when I didn't have to.   —T. R.

✪ Make a new friend
❑ Host a "friends of friends" party
❑ Contact old friends
❑ Have a friend who doesn't leave
❑ Meet other moms
❑ Make friends with his friends
❑ Join a softball league
❑ Make new friends at my new school

Don't let family get in the way of friendships

Chaperoning the middle school dance or coaching weekend soccer games (along with a million other parental responsibilities) leaves little time for making new friends. Here are some ways to cultivate grown-up relationships:

- Host a dinner party and hire babysitters to entertain guests' wee ones with movies, books, and games in a back bedroom.

- Designate one or more nights a month as standing dates to meet friends for a movie, dinner out, or an evening of dancing. Building friend-time into your family routine means it's one less thing to think about *and* you can book your babysitters well in advance.

- Arrange to meet other parents at hip, kid-friendly events such as Baby Loves Disco (www.babylovesdisco.com), which hosts afternoon dance parties at local clubs across the country where parents and half pints can groove to hits from the '70s and '80s.

❑ Join the PTA
❑ Invite neighbors in for coffee
❑ Become friends with my sister

✪ Figure out where all the people like me are hiding

❑ Form a knitting group in my neighborhood
❑ Arrange more play dates for my kids
❑ Have a foreign friend

✪ Be more social

❑ Join a church
❑ Join a fraternity
❑ Improve my conversation skills
❑ Become friends with my mom
❑ Don't be afraid to go out to bars alone
❑ Have a friend from another state
❑ Join a community garden

> ## "I got more involved in my neighborhood."
>
> We walk the dogs, deliver the neighborhood newsletter, attend general meetings, read and post to the neighborhood Listserv, attend art studio tours, plant trees, go to neighborhood parties, and attend the elementary school's events. We moved in just over a year ago, and I already know more people here than I did after living in my previous house for almost ten years. —C. U.

- ❑ Join a bowling league
- ❑ Go out with some of my coworkers
- ❑ Join a flag football team
- ❑ Become friends with my best friend all over again
- ✪ **Leave the house more**
- ❑ Make new sober friends
- ❑ Attend more social events
- ✪ **Be friends with my ex**

Start a cooking club

Cooking clubs are a great way to get to know acquaintances, coworkers, or friends of friends because there is a shared interest, a built-in-activity, and a conversation starter—making food. Cooking clubs involve making a dinner together, and hosting one means choosing the menu and providing the necessary tools and ingredients. Choosing simple entrées such as build-your-own pizza, gives guests more time to gab, whereas more sophisticated recipes force guests to interact as a team—chopping, mixing, and assembling delectable dishes. For more tips, recipe ideas, and quick-and-easy checklists, visit the Bon Appétit Cooking Club site (www.bonappetit.com/magazine/cookingclub).

"I befriended a stranger."

I saw this woman at the airport indoor play area (like her, I was seeing my husband off on a business trip). She was one of the most strikingly beautiful women I've ever seen. Not a model type, but with a true beauty that seemed to come from inside her. I went up and said, "You are one of the most beautiful women I have ever seen." I think she understood I was sincere and not a weirdo. We talked for some time and exchanged numbers. A friendship developed, and she later told me that she had been so sad that day and hearing that compliment helped her get through the day. You never know how important your words can be even to a stranger.

—J.D.C.

❑ Start a wine-tasting group
❑ Sit at a stranger's table at a restaurant and start a conversation
❑ Become friends with my roommate
❑ Join a running club
❑ Be the first to say "Hello"

20

"Nature's peace will flow into
you as sunshine flows into trees.
The winds will blow their own
freshness into you, and the storms
their energy, while cares will
drop off like autumn leaves."

—*John Muir, naturalist*

Enjoy **Nature**

Imagine sunlight streaming through a canopy of towering redwood trees. The soothing sounds of a river rushing over stones. The chirp of birds, the rustle of leaves, the sweep of a horizon that stretches on forever. It's the great outdoors—it's right outside your window, and it's wondering where you've been. Any nature lover will tell you that to ignore the majesty of the natural world is to forget that we're all part of a complex and beautiful system. Find ways to connect with nature by camping, hiking, and kayaking. Or celebrate closer to home and transform your backyard into a wildlife sanctuary. Or simply watch the sun set each evening from your bedroom window. All of these goals will serve to remind you that you are part of something much larger than yourself.

- ❏ Spend as much time outdoors as I do indoors
- ❏ Picnic in a country meadow
- ❏ Plant a fruit tree
- ❏ Take a kayak to the middle of the lake and just sit there
- ✪ **Catch fireflies**
- ❏ Ride an elephant in India
- ❏ Go whale watching
- ❏ Plant my own garden
- ❏ Sleep under the stars
- ❏ Enjoy the first snowfall

"I've seen the northern lights."

I grew up in a small town in northern Ontario. I used to stay up at night just staring out my window watching the lights dance across the sky. Red, green, blue, orange, yellow, fast, slow. Never the same, always changing, so amazing. I encourage you to do whatever you can to see them. And do not settle for the faint, crappy green ones. Go for the real deal—the ones that look like curtains hanging from heaven. The best is when there are two different colors and they dance like sheets drying on the clothesline on a breezy day. So beautiful! —M. T.

- ❏ Create an outdoor room for sleeping in the summer
- ❏ Visit Japan in autumn and see the maple leaves turn red
- ❏ Camp out on a beach
- ❏ Swim with sea turtles
- ❏ Eat a fresh fig
- ❏ Jump into a pile of leaves
- ❏ Place an owl box in my garden
- ❏ Visit the Redwood Forest
- ❏ Find a four-leaf clover
- ❏ Walk through an orchard
- ❏ Live where the air is fresh
- ❏ Skip stones across a lake
- ✪ **Plant a rose garden**
- ❏ Buy land in the country
- ❏ Spend vacation time preserving wildlife
- ❏ Put up bat houses
- ❏ Lie in the sun and watch autumn leaves fall
- ❏ Grow an African violet from a leaf cutting
- ❏ Backpack in "big sky" country
- ✪ **Grow sunflowers**
- ❏ Feed a giraffe
- ❏ Plant a tree right in the heart of a metropolis
- ❏ Build a pond in my backyard and stock it with fish

"I hiked into the Grand Canyon."

First, I day-hiked in about one mile. It was so amazing—and rather intimidating!—to watch the ancient canyon walls rise up around me as I descended. The next hike was longer in distance and duration. We packed our stuff and walked out to Horseshoe Mesa to camp. When we arrived at the mesa, rather than just frolicking about and exploring, I focused on finding a spot that felt good and hunkered down away from the wind and cold and watched the world slowly change from day to evening to night. The stars were some of the best I've seen, including a number of incredible shooters. In the morning I took a walk out to the end of the mesa and got an incredible view of the inner canyon.   —O. V.

❏ Feel the grass between my toes
❏ Stargaze in the desert
❏ Watch a hummingbird
✪ **Experience snow for the first time**
❏ Visit the ocean once a year
❏ Always have fresh flowers in my house
❏ Kayak in Glacier Bay
❏ Sit outside during a spring storm
❏ Fly-fish in Alaska

❑ Move far away from the city, to live close
to nature

❑ Eat a piece of fruit right from the tree

❑ See a real wolf

Create a backyard habitat for wildlife

Making your backyard inviting for wildlife helps the
environment, beautifies your property, and gives you a way
to enjoy nature at home. Just follow these steps:

- Plant native trees and shrubs to provide a food source
  and install feeders for hummingbirds, squirrels, and
  butterflies.

- Build a pond or place birdbaths in the yard as a source
  of clean water.

- Give various species places to raise their young or to
  escape from predators, such as bushy shrubs, piles of
  small logs or rocks, a roosting box, or a birdhouse.

- Abstain from using any pesticides or herbicides to
  preserve the quality of the soil, water, and air, and
  employ sustainable gardening techniques such as
  mulching and collecting water in rain barrels.

For more details about backyard habitats, go to the
National Wildlife Federation website at www.nwf.org.

- ❏ Watch the sky and wait for a falling star
- ❏ Join an outdoor adventure club
- ❏ Collect stones by the sea
- ❏ Chase the shadow of a high-flying eagle
- ❏ Witness a total solar eclipse
- ❏ Play in a field of wild lupine
- ❏ Have a nap in the shade of a tree
- ❏ Feed a squirrel
- ❏ Get lost in a forest
- ❏ Photograph wildlife
- ❏ Plant a tree on Arbor Day
- ✪ **Camp in the desert**
- ❏ Walk down to the ocean at least twice a week
- ❏ See a shark in the wild
- ❏ Dive the kelp forest in Monterey
- ✪ **Climb a mountain**
- ❏ Meditate under a waterfall
- ❏ Walk barefoot in the park
- ❏ See the Earth from outer space
- ❏ Live in the mountains
- ❏ Take a picture of the sky every day
- ❏ Go canoeing
- ❏ Kayak among orcas
- ❏ Snorkel in a coral reef

Become a bird-watcher

In the world of bird-watching, the term *life list* takes on a different meaning. Birders keep track of species they have identified by maintaining a "life list" documenting the location, date, and type of bird. Identifying birds based on their song, colors, and features is a challenge you can enjoy at any age, and some birds, like the ivory-billed woodpecker, are so rare that it's a lifetime accomplishment to see one in the wild. Here are a few tips on how to get started:

- Purchase a pair of lightweight binoculars with a magnification of 6–8 in power
- Buy a field guide that provides diagrams of birds' markings, body shapes, and beaks, and range maps showing areas where certain birds are common. (Peterson Field Guides is a popular series.)
- Go bird-watching early in the morning when the proverbial "early bird" is out catching the worm, and remember to remain absolutely quiet when watching.
- Learn from experienced birders by signing up for an Audubon Society tour or joining a local bird-watching group. A great online resource is available at www.birding.com.

> ## "I swam in a bioluminescent bay."
>
> I dove into the cold water, and it was like swimming through the stars. With my nearsightedness, size and distance were indistinct; the light swirling off my fingertips was clouds and fog, universes and nebulas.　　—L. F.

- ❑ Recognize at least 5 constellations
- ✪ **Sleep in a tree**
- ❑ Go midnight horseback riding
- ❑ Camp in Yellowstone National Park
- ❑ Study biology in a rain forest
- ❑ Plant a tree with my children
- ❑ Scuba dive with dolphins
- ❑ Plant flowers in window boxes
- ❑ See a buffalo
- ❑ Kayak in the Galápagos
- ❑ Pet a seal
- ❑ Live by the ocean
- ❑ Have a picnic in Joshua Tree National Park
- ❑ Go for nature walks on the weekend
- ❑ Put up bat houses
- ✪ **Camp at Yosemite**
- ❑ Spend at least an hour a day outside

❑ Watch a thunderstorm

❑ Walk on a glacier

✪ **Watch the sunrise**

❑ Build a fairy house on Monhegan Island

❑ Swim in the ocean

❑ Go on a horseback-riding safari in Botswana

❑ Watch the sunset each evening

❑ Dive the Great Barrier Reef

❑ Run through a field of wildflowers

❑ Ride a camel

❑ Go into the countryside after a rain and inhale the delicious aroma of wet soil

Take a hike

Public parks are good hiking options, but the following locations get high marks for their breathtaking scenery:

- Pacific Crest Trail in California's High Sierra
- Glacier Gorge at Rocky Mountain National Park in Colorado
- Bear Mountain at Mount Riga State Park in Connecticut
- Black Mountain Crest in North Carolina's Mount Mitchell State Park
- Taylor River Trail at Big Creek Falls in Washington

21

"To a new world of gods and monsters!"

—*Dr. Septimus Pretorius in* Bride of Frankenstein

Develop **Supernatural** Powers

A century ago, the idea of sending people into outer space, wirelessly videoconferencing across the globe, or performing laser surgeries was considered the stuff of science fiction. And today, even preposterous-sounding ideas such as android armies, orbital hotels, and floating cities are possible if you can afford the multimillion- and billon-dollar price tags. So who's to say that levitating and teleporting aren't feasible? You don't have to twiddle your thumbs waiting for modern science to catch up with science fiction. If you find the idea of the paranormal ridiculous, try being less critical and more creative by envisioning something fantastical that transcends the present-day limitations. Because all you need to achieve the seemingly impossible is your imagination.

- ❏ Stop a train with my bare hands
- ❏ Turn water into wine
- ❏ Fly
- ❏ Find a way to travel faster than the speed of light
- ❏ Breathe fire
- ❏ Be Spider-Man
- ❏ Gain superhuman powers from eating something from a malfunctioning microwave
- ✪ **Levitate**
- ❏ Bring dead people back to life
- ❏ Be Superwoman
- ❏ Wiggle my nose to travel from one place to another (just like on *Bewitched*)
- ❏ Learn pyrokinesis

Hypnotize others

You don't need supernatural abilities to hypnotize someone, but hypnosis does give you the power of mind control, so use it responsibly. Learn how to hypnotize an individual by following instructions available at HypnosisNow.com or enrolling in a course at the Hypnotherapy Academy of America (www.hypnotherapyacademy.com).

"I am a superhero."

Behold, Captain Cubicle! You can become your own superhero (or villain, or neutral character) at Comic Vine (www.comicvine.com). The site is actually something of a Wikipedia of comic books, creators, storylines, powers, and places. Registering for the site lets you create your own superbeing's personality. By writing and editing descriptions on the site (there's lots of empty space for lesser-known comics), you are awarded points that determine your status as a superbeing. Right now, mine puts me slightly above a Boy Scout helping Granny cross the street.

—S. S.

❑ Become Aquaman
❑ Lift a car
❑ Be Supergirl
❑ Shape-shift
✪ **Learn telepathy**
❑ Communicate with animals
❑ Break a board with my hand
❑ Talk to the dead
❑ Become immortal
❑ Shoot lasers out of my eyes

Learn telekinesis

Who wouldn't want to move objects with their mind? Although there have been notable demonstrations of telekinetic ability, such events are still officially considered hoaxes. But many people remain dedicated to proving that telekinesis is possible and the RetroPsychoKinesis Project has online tests and training tools available to develop your ability to move objects with your mind. To participate in retropsychokinesis online experiments go to www.fourmilab.ch/rpkp. Or practice using your mind to influence matter, time, space, or energy at Learn-Telekinesis-Training.com, an online forum of individuals working to develop telekinesis.

❑ Control the weather
❑ Be omnipotent
❑ Possess the power of body elasticity
❑ Have Wolverine's powers
❑ Come back from the dead
❑ Be unbreakable
❑ Dodge bullets
❑ Become a vampire
❑ Command lightning

- ❑ Be invisible
- ❑ Be Superman
- ❑ Be able to generate sounds beyond normal human amplitude
- ❑ Breathe underwater
- ❑ Become a mutant with superpowers
- ❑ Get X-ray vision
- ❑ Be a mermaid
- ❑ Transform myself into a superhuman cyborg
- ❑ Freeze time

"I saved someone's life (even though I'm not a superhero)."

The light had just changed for us to cross the street. As this girl in a lab coat stepped off the curb to cross, I caught a glimpse of a car barreling toward us at 60 mph and fully intent on running the red light. In that split second my brain said, "she's going to die." I reached out and grabbed a fistful of the back of her lab coat and yanked her back from the oncoming car. *Whoosh*. The car sped past, missing her by fractions of an inch. She looked back at me, not realizing how close she had come to instant death. Everyone on the corner waiting to cross told her how lucky she was.   —S. Y.

Look what's coming!

The U.S. Department of Defense's Advanced Research Projects Agency (DARPA) solicits and funds far-fetched technologies that could eventually reach the commercial market. (DARPA was responsible for bringing computer scientists together to create an early prototype of the Internet.) Take a look at the projects they're working on these days:

- A way to fully regenerate the function of muscles, nerves, skin, and other complex tissue after a traumatic injury—essentially, the power to heal immediately, like X-Man Wolverine.
- Highly efficient, human-powered swimming devices using a new concept in swimming propulsion modeled after the movement of fish and aquatic birds. Strap on scuba gear and this gizmo, and you're Aquaman.

❑ Get a cape and fly around the world
❑ Discover that I can control others with my thoughts
✪ **Become a werewolf**
❑ Be able to locate things using echolocation
❑ Heal the sick

❑ Create electricity with my bare hands
❑ Make a voodoo doll of my ex
❑ Be able to teleport
❑ Possess the ability to take on animal forms
❑ Form a rainbow with my mind
❑ Discover the origin of life
❑ Be someone's guardian angel
❑ Stake a vampire
❑ Witness an exorcism
❑ Be able to transform into a gaseous foglike form
❑ Have an out-of-body experience
❑ Master lucid dreaming
❑ Survive a flood, a plague, or a locust invasion
❑ Perform a miracle
❑ Live through an earthquake
❑ Be a prophet
❑ Have a religion formed around my existence
❑ Experience divine intervention
❑ Escape from a straitjacket submerged in water
❑ Walk through a brick wall
❑ Read my fiancé's mind

22

"I used to be so spontaneous, but work and responsibilities had been sucking the life out of me. I rarely got out and I hardly did anything new or exciting. I have since changed my ways and slowly I have started to rediscover life and myself." —R. E., 43 Things member

Get Out More

There's a big, wide world outside your door, and where are you? You're inside with a long list of excuses: too much work, too many chores, no money, gross weather. It's time to get out and enjoy life, so shut down your computer, turn off the TV, and get out of the house. Invite friends out to lunch, visit a museum, or relive your childhood at an amusement park. Take a frugal approach to entertainment and feed bread to ducks at the park. And remember, no matter how many back-to-back meetings are on the calendar, you can always squeeze in a fifteen-minute walk around the block. You'll discover that the simple act of engaging in new activities, enjoying others' company, or just getting a little change of scenery every now and again has the power to reinvigorate your life.

- ❑ Take morning walks
- ❑ Attend a gala event or charity benefit dressed to the nines
- ❑ Try a new restaurant once a month
- ❑ Say yes to all invitations
- ✪ **Attend a film festival**
- ❑ Drink tea in a Japanese tea garden
- ❑ Leave the office for lunch every day
- ❑ Take a cake-decorating class
- ❑ Visit an amusement park
- ❑ Go to the movies once a week

"I've started to play tennis."

Finally! It's been on my New Year's resolution list for the last fifteen years! Tennis is the only thing that can get me out for one or two hours straight on a weeknight after a long day of work or shuttling my daughter around. Afterward, I have more energy and it's a real stress buster. (I hit that ball so hard sometimes, it's like someone's name is written on it.) I love the feeling when I am all warmed up and catching my second wind. I love not giving up and going after every shot. I love how focused it makes me and how fun it is to play.

—M. A.

- ❑ Attend a yoga workshop
- ❑ Spend an entire day in the bookstore reading philosophy books
- ❑ Go to a comedy club
- ❑ Visit more public gardens
- ❑ Go bowling
- ❑ Take a silversmithing class

✪ **Spend more time outside**

- ❑ Have a standing date with my friends at least every two months
- ❑ Visit a candy factory
- ❑ Spend a day driving in the mountains
- ❑ Take a massage class
- ❑ Sing in the rain
- ❑ Go roller skating around my block
- ❑ Attend a concert of every musical genre

✪ **Spend a day at a spa**

- ❑ Take a woodworking class
- ❑ Get season tickets to my community theater and *go*
- ❑ Attend a poetry reading
- ❑ Visit a flea market

✪ **Go fishing**

- ❑ Spend a day sailing
- ❑ Go to more lectures

- ☐ Have a picnic at sunrise
- ☐ Meet an old friend for coffee
- ☐ Leave the office for lunch
- ☐ Visit an art gallery
- ✪ **Go to the beach**
- ☐ Attend a midnight screening of
  The Rocky Horror Picture Show
- ✪ **Play basketball**
- ☐ Walk in the snow at night
- ☐ Attend the opera
- ☐ Visit a planetarium
- ☐ Go to a hockey game
- ☐ Spend an afternoon at the library

Go stargazing

Lying in the backyard or on the roof and gazing at the stars is cheap, easy, and you don't have to shower, dress up, or travel far from home. If light pollution is a problem, then pack a blanket and head to the outskirts of town for the nighttime show. But before you take it all in, read about the constellations and celestial events at the following websites: StarDate.org, NightSkyInfo.com, or Space.com. You might even want to print out a star map and take it with you.

> ## "I take a walk each evening."
>
> Just got back from another one of my exhilarating walks.
> I even went out of my way to climb a steep hill. The clouds
> were absolutely incredible and dark gray until the sun
> pierced through and turned them golden. It's nice to find
> little things to appreciate each evening.   —N. C.

❑ Sit in a café and people-watch

✪ **See a play**

❑ Tour a pretzel factory

❑ Take a jewelry-making class

❑ Pick wild berries

✪ **Go to more museums**

❑ Go on a camping trip with my friends

❑ Play bingo

❑ Spend a day gallery hopping

❑ Do yard work for 30 minutes a day

❑ Take a flower-arranging class

❑ Visit the countryside

❑ Go swimming

❑ Look for secret hiding places and beautiful views
on my bike

❑ Take a sewing class

Be a tourist in your own town

Even if you've lived in the same town since you were born, consider spending a day playing tourist to get a fresh perspective on the place you thought you knew best. Sign up for a walking tour of the historic district or visit the so-called "tourist traps" you've always avoided. Poke around the local historical society and uncover some long-forgotten town scandals or photos of Main Street before the strip malls took over. Your library may have a special shelf of books by local authors and artists that can place your town in a whole new light. Bring a friend along and take pictures of each other in front of your favorite landmarks—whether it's a statue of the town's founder or the Dunkin' Donuts where you get your daily joe. Sure, it may not be Paris, but it is home.

❑ Set up a croquet set and invite neighbors over to play
❑ Spend an entire day building a massive sand castle
✪ **Ride my bike more**
❑ Attend a wine-tasting event
❑ Spend a day taking pictures

- ❏ Visit the zoo
- ❏ Rent a plot in a community garden
- ❏ Take Sunday bike rides
- ❏ Feed the ducks
- ❏ Spend an entire day people-watching
- ✪ **Take a photography class**
- ❏ Spend the day being a kid again
- ❏ Attend a symphony concert
- ❏ Go out every night for a whole week
- ❏ Attend a fashion show
- ❏ Spend the day downtown with friends
- ❏ Go out for afternoon tea
- ❏ Take horseback-riding lessons
- ❏ Have lunch with a friend

> ## "I'm taking a martial arts class."
>
> I've wanted to do this since I was eleven years old, and twenty years later, I'm in my second week of tae kwon do. I am the second-oldest white belt in the class (the newest white belt is in her seventies) and I feel like a kid during recess! The exercises and drills have motivated me to get to the gym more to build up stamina. I have more confidence already, and it just feels good! —N. E.

Organize a "track and field day" for your grown-up friends

Invite friends to the schoolyard or park, form teams, appoint refs and timekeepers, and even award medals during a closing ceremony. Guarantee a fun time regardless of athletic ability with some of these events:

- In an open field, draw start and finish lines and hold old-fashioned relay games such as the baton pass, sack race, and three-legged race.

- Hold a hula hoop contest and judge who can hula hoop the longest without stopping.

- For the long-jump event, stretch out a measuring tape and secure both ends in a soft grassy area or sand pit. Contestants will stand on a line and jump as far as they can.

- Measure out 100 meters in an open field or parking lot for the 100-meter dash. Have runners line up one at a time, and use a stopwatch to time each person.

- Fill balloons with water, tie off the ends, and have two-person teams toss them back and forth until the balloons pop. The last team with an intact water balloon wins.

❑ Start a playgroup for my kids
❑ Take a gymnastics class
❑ Spend the day at the races
❑ Check out my local lawn-bowling club
❑ Go on a pub crawl
❑ Join a flag football team
❑ Join my neighborhood association
❑ Tour an ice cream factory
❑ Do my shopping at a farmers' market
✪ **Hear more live music**
❑ Play chess with the guys in the park
❑ Spend a day working on a farm
❑ Go to a playground and play on all the equipment
❑ Take a letterpress class
❑ Go out for drinks and play pub trivia
❑ Spend a day by the pool
❑ Go for a sleigh ride
❑ Have a picnic in the park
✪ **Go to a professional football game**
❑ Take a brewery tour

23

"I have often reflected upon the new vistas that reading opened to me. As I see it today, the ability to read awoke in me some long dormant craving to be mentally alive." —*Malcom X*

Read More

Books are simple physical objects. Crisp white pages, bound with glue or thread, line after line of words in plain black type, and in them an entire world. Paperback novels that transport and thrill, historical tomes that illuminate and explain, hardbound volumes of poetry that sing—all held between your two hands. For those who haven't opened a book since college, consider this: An appetite for books is just like any other—consume the wrong thing at the wrong time and it doesn't sit right, but find just what you're looking for and it's bliss. Awaken your inner bookworm and read the things that excite you, not things you think you *should* read. And for those of you on a first-name basis with the librarian, give a word of thanks that something so simple can give you so much.

- ☐ Spend more time reading books than I spend on the Internet
- ☐ Read something spiritual every day
- ☐ Read books written by authors from my hometown
- ☐ Read only books by female authors for the next year
- ☐ Read every book I own
- ✪ **Visit my local library**
- ☐ Read the fundamental Buddhist texts
- ☐ Carry a paperback book to read throughout the day
- ☐ Read more works from the Beat Generation
- ☐ Swap reading lists with friends

"I read to my kids."

My mom used to read to my sister, brother, and me every night. That's when I learned to love reading. When I was old enough to read, my mom would sit and listen to me read her a story. I loved all the different places you could go, the people you could be, and the things you could learn from books. I want my children to love books and learning as much as I did.

—P. S.

- ❏ Read the newspaper every day
- ❏ Improve my knowledge of geography and history through books
- ❏ Make a list of my all-time favorite books and reread them
- ❏ Learn to speed-read
- ❏ Read books other than romance novels
- ✪ **Go to a poetry reading**
- ❏ Read erotic fiction
- ❏ Read my favorite books from childhood to my children
- ❏ Read on the beach
- ❏ Listen to more audio books
- ❏ Read books on the subway
- ✪ **Make a summer reading list**
- ❏ Read more novels
- ❏ Reread my old Nancy Drew books
- ❏ Form a vampire poetry group
- ❏ Read all the books I should have read in college
- ✪ **Spend more time reading than watching TV**
- ❏ Read *The Odyssey*
- ❏ Have a collection of all my favorite books, in hardback
- ❏ Read magazines

Delve into the literature of Nobel Prize winners

Since 1901, the Nobel Prize in Literature has honored authors who have spent their lifetime producing works that better the world through their artistry. Recent winners have included a diverse and powerful group of writers whose books will challenge and inspire:

- Doris Lessing has written about politics and race relations, and is best known for her early feminist work *The Golden Notebook*.
- Orhan Pamuk, one of Turkey's bestselling novelists, is a champion of free speech and the author of *My Name Is Red* and *Snow*.
- Harold Pinter is an overtly political British playwright and poet whose works often express outrage over state-sponsored wars and explore themes of power struggles.
- Elfriede Jelinek, a lesser-known Austrian novelist, writes books that speak out against sexual violence, oppression, and right-wing extremism.
- J. M. Coetzee is a South African novelist who explores the human condition through the lens of apartheid.

- ❏ Go to a café and read a poem aloud
- ❏ Read all the great American authors
- ✪ **Read more philosophy**
- ❏ Read *Don Quixote* in the original Spanish
- ❏ Read more critically
- ❏ Read to the sick or elderly at hospitals and nursing homes
- ❏ Read more contemporary authors
- ❏ Buy an eBook reader
- ❏ Read everything by Dr. Seuss
- ❏ Read and see all of Shakespeare's plays
- ❏ Read Nietzsche

"I set my books free."

I want to leave my finished books around town in various places where someone else will find them and enjoy them. Just leaving the book means that someone else finds it and owns it, but I want them to pass it on and on and on. I have a simple instruction card taped to the front cover so that the next "owner" will know what to do with the book once they've finished reading it. I just finished reading Richard Wright's *Native Son*, which I bought at the library for $0.10. Sometime this week, I'll set it free.   — O. V.

Read more poetry

Often overlooked by readers, poetry can be one of the most pleasurable and mesmerizing forms of storytelling: a quiet moment, a turn of passion, a childhood memory condensed into a few lines of taut, powerful language. Somewhere between a prayer and a song, poems require you to read carefully, allowing layers of meaning to reveal themselves with each subsequent reading. Start small with a poem a day from Poetry Daily (www.poems.com) or pick up *The Norton Anthology of Poetry,* open to any page, and start reading.

❑ Be able to recite 10 poems from memory
❑ Read more plays
❑ Host a book swap
❑ Read every book in my library
❑ Read more academic journals
✪ **Read a trashy romance novel**
❑ Read books with my son at night
❑ Set aside an hour to read each day
❑ Read the dictionary
❑ Read more mysteries
✪ **Read the book before I see the movie**
❑ Read *The Divine Comedy* in Italian

❑ Read a novel aloud with a friend
❑ Read in bed every night before sleep
✪ **Read more biographies**
❑ Read a graphic novel
❑ Improve my reading skills
❑ Read all the works of my favorite author
❑ Organize an author reading series at my local bookstore or library
✪ **Read all the great Russian authors**
❑ Start a book club that reads only epics
❑ Have a library of books in my house
❑ Stage a reading of my favorite play

"I learned from *The Lord of the Rings*."

The Lord of the Rings gave me far more than just a great read: It formed a large part of my sense of ethics and how I make sense of the world. Because of *The Lord of the Rings* I know the value of mercy, the nobility of honor, the strength in selfless sacrifice. This book infused me with the eternal conviction that Right and Wrong really do matter, and Right may have a hard time of it, but in the long term will triumph.

—E. L.

Start a reading group

Book clubs direct you to books you might otherwise overlook and spark challenging discussions that get you thinking and reading critically. They're also a great excuse to spend an evening with some friends and good snacks. A few tips to keep your meetings fresh:

- Make sure you have enough time between meetings for everyone to finish the book. People are busy and if they have to rush to finish, the reading group will become more of a burden than a pleasure.

- For each meeting, select a facilitator to lead the discussion. The facilitator should come prepared with questions to get the conversation started, some information about the author, and reviews of the book.

- If possible, invite an author to meet with your group, or attend readings at local bookstores as a group.

- Keep reading groups fresh with reading guides, discussion topics, and other ideas from Book-Clubs-Resource.com or LitLovers.com. Or check out the *Utne Reader* guide to hosting a salon (www.utne.com).

❏ Read my kid's entire comic book collection
❏ Read the original reviews of my favorite old books
❏ Read one nonfiction book a month
❏ Read an entire book in a cozy corner of a bookstore
✪ **Read all the Pulitzer Prize–winning novels**
❏ Finish reading half-read books
❏ Translate Spanish poems into English
❏ Read one book each week for a year
❏ Study the Greek and Roman classics
❏ Read books in their original languages

24

"Imagination is more important than knowledge." —*Albert Einstein*

Create

Being creative isn't about making a masterpiece.
In fact, it's not really about outcomes at all.
Being creative is about process—it's about
letting your imagination take you on an
exhilarating ride with every ounce of your
attention so caught up in the moment that the
hours slip away like minutes. Don't wait around
for divine inspiration or a visit from the Greek
muses. Get out your watercolors and try to
capture the light in your garden. Sketch a design
and silk-screen it on a T-shirt. Or simply cut up
old magazines and glue the words and photos
into a collage to hang in your bedroom. Create
something from nothing—the finished product
could be terrifying or terrific, but the experience
is guaranteed to be thrilling.

- ❑ Sketch one thing every day
- ✪ **Play, record, mix, and produce my own music**
- ❑ Design my own tattoo
- ❑ Host a jack-o'-lantern carving competition with friends
- ❑ Fill every notebook I own with new ideas
- ❑ Make a sock monkey
- ❑ Learn how to blow glass beads
- ✪ **Write a children's book**
- ❑ Refashion a really funky T-shirt
- ❑ Publish a coffee table book of my photography
- ❑ Design lingerie
- ❑ Shoot a documentary film
- ❑ Learn to silk-screen like Andy Warhol
- ❑ Master painting with acrylics
- ❑ Create and name a new color
- ❑ Make homemade candles
- ❑ Design and build a luxury dollhouse
- ❑ Publish my own songs
- ❑ Hand-bind a selection of my original poetry
- ❑ Crochet an afghan
- ❑ Play with crayons and play dough like I did when I was a kid

> ## "I made a collage."
>
> I'm not really the artsy-craftsy type, but I found this very satisfying—deciding on the theme, selecting the components (words, images, colors), the cutting, the arranging on the page, the gluing, the painting and coloring. It took me back to those days in elementary school, with glue and paint and paper and crayons and poster board and those little child-safe round-tipped scissors; it made me feel creative and it was very therapeutic. —T. L.

❑ Design and make my own jewelry

❑ Paint a mural on my bedroom wall

✪ **Landscape my yard**

❑ Design roller coasters

❑ Make a picture frame out of a tin ceiling tile

❑ Make cloth dolls for my kids

✪ **Make a mix tape**

❑ Curate an exhibition at a gallery

❑ Turn my apartment into a space where I can be creative

❑ Design and print my own stationery

❑ Make a papier-mâché mask

❑ Design a stencil and go tagging

Rediscover the joys of sidewalk chalk

Sidewalk chalk isn't just for the under-ten set, it's used by artists around the world to create ephemeral works of art. Whether you re-create a Picasso or doodle a portrait of your dog, transforming dull concrete with vibrant colors is a great way to reconnect with the easy creativity of youth. Here are some ideas to get you started:

- Invent an elaborate hopscotch course: twenty-six squares, extra points given for triple jumps and cartwheels.
- Gather friends and collaborate on drawing a fantastical train, using a whole sidewalk square for each new car.
- Write a neighborhood-long poem that wraps around multiple blocks, with each person adding a new line, having read only the previous line.
- *Some general tips:* Sweep the area where you'll be working. Fix mistakes or soften designs with a chalkboard eraser, and make drawings last longer by spraying the finished product with aerosol hairspray.

❏ Knit baby booties
❏ Design my own sarongs
❏ Create a mosaic

✪ **Publish a book**

❑ Invent my own sandwich

❑ Start a guerilla art campaign

❑ Work on my novel

❑ Design a line of toys

❑ Collaborate with someone on an art installation

❑ Build my own kitchen table out of reclaimed wood

✪ **Sew my own clothes**

❑ Finger paint the walls of a room

❑ Make a living from my art

❑ Print a book with a letterpress

❑ Make a duct tape wallet

✪ **Write a story**

❑ Design sneakers for a living

"I created something beautiful."

Maybe it's arrogant, but I truly think that some of the paintings I've done recently are, if not beautiful, close to it. There's nothing more satisfying than creating something on your own. Taking nothing but canvases and paints, dirt and seeds, ingredients, whatever, and turning them into something breathtaking is the most rewarding thing you can do.   —M.M.B.

Make your own wrapping paper

Express your creativity, impress friends and family, and pinch pennies by transforming butcher and wax paper into unique gift wrap.

Arrange dried leaves or flowers on a piece of wax paper. Lay a second piece of wax paper on top. Use an iron on a low-heat setting to melt the pieces of wax paper together. Wrap gifts first in white butcher paper and then a second time with the decorative wax paper. For wedding or holiday gifts, sprinkle glitter over the flowers and leaves.

❑ Create a logo
✪ **Be confident in the art I make**
❑ Knit legwarmers
❑ Paint more with oils
❑ Choreograph a dance
❑ Make a stained-glass panel
❑ Make my own picture frames
❑ Design my own wallpaper
❑ Publish a book of songs
❑ Create an indestructible chew toy for my dog
❑ Create a famous ad campaign
❑ Make a ceramic vase

- ❏ Create my own fragrance
- ❏ Make a Wonder Woman costume
- ✪ **Sew a skirt**
- ❏ Design and construct sailboats
- ❏ Build my own spaceship
- ❏ Weave a pot holder on a loom
- ❏ Invent a board game
- ❏ Design and manufacture an electric harmonica
- ✪ **Paint a self-portrait**
- ❏ Make a tutu
- ❏ Design my own jeans
- ❏ Refashion vintage necklaces
- ❏ Write a cookbook
- ❏ Design shoes
- ❏ Make my own essential oils

"I embroidered a baby blanket for my son."

I started before he was born. I got a soft blue blankie and embroidered his full name and some hearts in the corner. He was wrapped in it when we took him home from the hospital after he was born. Now he wraps his stuffed animals in it when they get cold. —S. A.

- ❑ Design my wedding ring
- ❑ Publish my own magazine
- ✪ **Illustrate a book**
- ❑ Throw a pot on a pottery wheel
- ❑ Make a rustic dining table from an old door
- ❑ Write a haiku every Friday
- ❑ Design handbags
- ❑ Direct a music video
- ❑ Invent a new sport
- ❑ Install ceramic tiles in my kitchen
- ❑ Cast a sculpture in bronze
- ❑ Create my own language
- ❑ Carve an ice sculpture
- ❑ Choreograph a modern dance
- ❑ Contribute to a 'zine
- ✪ **Develop a computer game**
- ❑ Quilt with my grandma
- ❑ Design and print business cards
- ❑ Write and direct a musical
- ❑ Draw my own Valentine's Day cards
- ✪ **Have my own art studio**
- ❑ Shoot a photo essay of the city I live in
- ❑ Make a Japanese-style lamp shade
- ❑ Press enough flowers to cover my ceiling

Tie-dye a T-shirt

Tie-dying is an easy and thrifty way to experiment with color, shape, and pattern. (It's messy, too, so stock up on garbage bags and rubber gloves.) Different twists will produce different results—instructions for specific designs can be found at Ritdye.com. Here are instructions for a three-color design:

1. Bind your fabric tightly into three equal sections using rubber bands.

2. Using three different fiber-reactive dyes (mixed per manufacturer's instructions), dip one outside section into one of the bowls of dye. Soak for about ten minutes (time may vary, depending on how saturated you want the color). Remove and rinse until the water runs clear.

3. Repeat with second outside section and a new color and then again with the middle section and the third color. Be careful not to let the colors run.

4. Let the fabric dry completely before removing rubber bands and washing it again in warm water with a mild detergent.

25

"You must be the change you wish to see in the world." —*Mahatma Gandhi*

Ignite Change

Shaping global agendas has to start somewhere—
why not with you? History is filled with stories
of ordinary people who changed the world
in extraordinary ways by recognizing a need,
believing in their abilities, and taking action.
Take your cues from these everyday folks who
mustered up the courage and fight to get out of
their armchairs and ignite change. Rather than
letting stacked odds, shoestring budgets, or red
tape deter their efforts, these individuals forged
ahead and transformed lives. Changing the world
is not about being perfect—it's about making a
commitment to becoming involved and invested.
It's about harnessing optimism, setting goals, and
having a purpose. Figure out how you think the
world could be a better place and then lead by
example.

- ☐ Change what seems impossible to change
- ✪ **Make my voice heard**
- ☐ Lobby for women's rights around the world
- ☐ Organize a student loan amnesty lobby
- ☐ Legalize tattoos in Oklahoma
- ☐ Support the United Nations Refugee Agency
- ☐ Write a manifesto
- ☐ Help single parents understand their rights
- ✪ **End poverty**
- ☐ Work for immigration reform
- ☐ Open my own public food pantry
- ☐ Participate in Rock the Vote

"I built schools in Kenya."

The experience was beyond amazing and a real eye-opener. It's definitely one thing to learn about poverty and another to see it firsthand. To see every single one of those schoolkids with yellow eyes from malnutrition and many with runny noses and dirty hands is absolutely heartbreaking; but at the same time they are all so excited to learn that you can't help but be filled with hope. I am so happy to have been able to help bring education to those kids with my own two hands.   —F.M.H.

✪ **Help find a cure for cancer**
- ❑ Participate in a peace protest
- ❑ Fight for social justice
- ❑ Volunteer as a human rights observer in Guatemala
- ❑ Ban guns
- ❑ Promote body acceptance
- ❑ Lobby to change legislation to help disabled vets
- ❑ Ban trashy television
- ❑ Abolish live-animal circuses
- ❑ Legalize marijuana
- ❑ Stand up for my rights
- ❑ Challenge homophobia in my school
- ❑ Lobby for insurance companies to cover infertility treatment
- ❑ Elect a third-party president
- ❑ Write a letter every week in support of my political causes

✪ **Strengthen public education**
- ❑ Start a 100 percent organic farmers' market
- ❑ Hold a public office
- ❑ Ban SUVs in cities
- ❑ Help to peacefully unseat world leaders who violate human rights
- ❑ Reform the public education system

- ❑ Legalize midwifery in all 50 states
- ✪ **Ban smoking in public places**
- ❑ Plan a fund-raiser for Darfur
- ❑ Advocate for prisoner's rights
- ❑ Change someone's mind for the better
- ❑ Ban people who want to ban things
- ❑ Work to find a cure for AIDS

Be a court-appointed special advocate

By joining Court Appointed Special Advocates, a volunteer network representing the interests of abused or neglected children in courtrooms across the country, you'll be providing a much needed support system for a child struggling with family problems, difficult circumstances, and the legal system. Anyone can apply to the program, and volunteers receive training in advocacy techniques, courtroom procedure, and adolescent behavior. Cases typically last one to two years, and advocates spend roughly twenty hours a month researching cases, attending legal proceedings to speak on a child's behalf, and generally watching out for the child's welfare. Apply to be a court-appointed advocate by searching www.nationalcasa.org to find a local program.

> ## "I started an orphanage in India."
>
> My wife and I were involved in starting an orphanage in India about four years ago. We are now on our way back to India to do it again. I've started a website dedicated to the establishment of orphanages at www.parentless.org. We can get you started down the road, and hopefully we can share ideas as we go.　　　　　—P. S.

❑ Lobby for a higher minimum wage
✪ **Influence future generations**
❑ Abolish the British monarchy
❑ Promote scientific literacy
❑ Work at the United Nations
❑ Develop a way to stop premature births
❑ Reform the education system in South Asia
❑ Wage peace
❑ Help create a national day care program
✪ **Advocate for universal health care**
❑ Influence public opinion
❑ Work to change U.S. foreign policy
❑ Raise awareness about global warming
❑ Be a political activist
❑ Campaign to end all animal testing

- ❏ Influence immigration regulations
- ❏ Abolish the electoral college
- ❏ Legalize prostitution
- ✪ **Create a secret society of optimists and do-gooders**
- ❏ Testify before Congress
- ❏ Film a documentary to raise awareness about the homeless
- ❏ Pass legislation to legalize gay marriage
- ✪ **Make the world a better place**
- ❏ Lobby city hall to make recycling mandatory in my town
- ❏ Start an underground newspaper
- ❏ Become a senator
- ❏ Help find a cure for Alzheimer's
- ❏ Work on a living-wage campaign
- ❏ Boycott stores that use factories with questionable labor practices
- ❏ Hold corporations responsible for environmental destruction
- ❏ Organize a forum on peace and justice
- ❏ Serve in the House of Representatives
- ✪ **Fight for civil rights**
- ❏ Change the juvenile justice system

Use the Internet for good

Thanks to the Internet and social networking websites, political movements are more accessible, and getting involved is easier than ever. Interact with people who share your concerns and engage with nonprofits by going to one of the following websites and donating or volunteering at your convenience:

- Change.org has thousands of ways for you to connect with grassroots networks and support causes ranging from ending global poverty to music programs for inner-city youth.
- Avaaz.org, a nonpartisan organization, offers tools to help you get involved with causes by filling out petitions and e-mailing lawmakers about climate change, religious conflicts, and other social issues.
- SpeakOut.com has tools to increase your political awareness such as discussion forums and debates and ways to get involved in political movements, including petition templates and online surveys.

❑ Do some consciousness raising on race in my community

❑ Fight for immigrant worker's rights

"I vote."

I feel very strongly about voting. Today, I tugged on my sneakers, grabbed my bag, and hiked the distance to the library. The polls were empty but for the volunteers, all of them elderly and all of them quite surprised to see me. When the woman asked me if I would like to review the amendments up for vote today, I was proud to be able to tell her that I had already read about them.

As I left, one of the volunteers pasted a small white sticker onto my shoulder. "I Voted," it proclaimed. As I strolled through my apartment complex, my head held high, some kids asked me about my sticker. I told them what a privilege voting is, how it makes a difference. The kids looked bored and somewhat amused, but maybe they will remember, and maybe the next generation will care more than mine. I hope so.   —F. G.

❑ Promote peace in the Middle East
❑ Start a youth social-justice arts organization
✪ **Support the American Civil Liberties Union**
❑ Promote gender equality
❑ Support independent businesses

✪ **Elect a woman as president**

❏ Start a cyclist advocacy campaign

❏ Throw a benefit concert to raise money for a cure for cancer

✪ **Open a homeless shelter**

❏ Volunteer in a refugee camp

❏ Advocate for those who have no voice

❏ Participate in a phone bank to "get out the vote"

❏ Initiate a moratorium on the death penalty

❏ Campaign for wind energy

❏ Raise money for Sudanese refugees

❏ Help the helpless

❏ Reform electoral practices in the United States

❏ Run for city council

❏ Advocate for renewable energy

❏ Volunteer at the International Refugee Committee

✪ **Reform the prison system**

❏ Buy a pair of breeding goats for a family in Rwanda

❏ Change the foster care system

❏ Become an advocate for children with autism

❏ Become a Supreme Court justice

❏ Campaign and raise money for research on mental illness

- ❏ Volunteer in Africa to fight the HIV/AIDS epidemic
- ❏ Organize a rally so big that the National Guard has to show up
- ❏ Unionize Wal-Mart
- ❏ Educate the public on climate change
- ❏ Be able to debate intelligently and passionately about politics
- ✪ **Win the Nobel Peace Prize**
- ❏ Work to save endangered species

Work to end homelessness

Helping the homeless is more than just donating a few dollars when you pass someone sleeping on the sidewalk or giving to shelters and charities. You can join numerous local and national organizations as a volunteer and help train homeless individuals for employment, work with a housing organization, or organize fund-raising events. Take action to help the homeless at the National Alliance to End Homelessness (www.endhomelessness.org), the Partnership to End Long-Term Homelessness (www.endlongtermhomelessness.org), or the National Coalition for the Homeless (www.nationalhomeless.org).

⊙ **Disarm the world of nuclear weapons**
❑ Empower people by teaching and by being
an example
❑ Stop the fur trade
❑ Open a free health clinic
❑ Reform the United States social welfare system
❑ Get green legislation enacted in my town
❑ Campaign to end female genital mutilation
❑ Open a school for child soldiers in Sudan
❑ Initiate a citywide movement to ban plastic
shopping bags
❑ Review every amendment on the ballot before
voting

26

"Never stay up on the barren heights of cleverness, but come down into the green valleys of silliness." —*Ludwig Wittgenstein*

Be Silly

Ever fantasize about throwing a handful of mashed potatoes at the person sitting at the next table? Maybe you're not into food fights, but we've all had that itch to do something ridiculous like launch a paper airplane off a skyscraper or swim in a vat of Jell-O. Silly, yes. But don't underestimate the power of silly— especially as a balance to life's more serious moments. Goofing off can be an antidote for the fun-robbing responsibilities that too often come with being a grown-up. So cut loose, be zany, and go crazy. Other people (and even you!) may snicker at your attempts to organize a water-balloon fight or wear fairy wings in public, but at least your life will be filled with laughter. And what could be a better stress-buster than laughing till you pee in your pants?

❑ Do a backflip
❑ Throw a pirate-themed wedding
❑ Be able to fake an Irish accent
✪ **Fly a kite**
❑ Take goofy pictures in a photo booth
❑ Have a pillow fight
❑ Bury a box of treasure
❑ Do a handstand
❑ Tell more jokes
❑ Dress like a penguin and slide in the snow
❑ Run through the sprinklers at night
✪ **Play spin the bottle**
❑ Moon someone from the side of the highway
❑ Slide down a banister
❑ Play hopscotch
❑ Climb trees in public places
❑ Play Twister drunk
❑ Twirl a baton
❑ Wear a mask in public
❑ Take silly pictures in front of landmarks
❑ Do a cartwheel
❑ Make breakfast for dinner
✪ **Make balloon animals**
❑ Wear a toga in Rome

"I made a snow angel."

There was a fresh layer of powder this morning, several inches deep and inviting; after I'd finished my morning chores, I flopped down in the snow and made a snow angel. The wind is always blowing on our little hill, so the snow I was kicking up whirled around my face and tickled my cheeks. The best part, though, was when the horse trotted out to the fence to laugh at the silly human in the snow. So worth it!   —G. H.

❑ Hula hoop in the middle of a crowded intersection

❑ Break into a musical number in public

❂ **Make a prank phone call**

❑ Roll down a sand dune

❑ Rent a hotel room and have a drunken underwear sleepover party

❑ Dance on a table

❑ Splash in puddles

❑ Organize a Slip 'n Slide party

❑ Throw a paper airplane off the top of the Empire State Building

❑ Blow bubbles in a mall

❑ Dress up as a ninja

✪ Color an entire coloring book

- ❏ Leave silly notes in the coin-return slots of soda machines
- ❏ Open an umbrella indoors
- ❏ Have a Silly String fight
- ❏ Skip down the middle of the street
- ❏ Serve sundaes for dinner
- ❏ Paint my nails in rainbow colors
- ❏ Take a bath in champagne
- ❏ Throw a pie-in-the-face party
- ❏ Jump off a waterfall in a rubber octopus suit
- ❏ Play more board games

Celebrate new holidays

Discover new reasons to celebrate with these happy holidays. Browse HolidayInsights.com for more wacky or whimsical ways to mark your calendar.

January 24—Compliment Day

April 14—International Moment of Laughter Day

May 6—International No Diet Day

June 6—National Yo-Yo Day

October 7—World Smile Day

November 13—World Kindness Day

"I walked through a drive-thru."

My friend and I went to McDonald's and pretended we had a car. I was the one "driving" and he was the "passenger." We had to walk while pretending to be sitting down. I mimed steering an invisible wheel and my friend squatted next to me. It was really busy and all these people were beeping at us. The server took one look at us—me with my arms outstretched, holding the wheel, and my friend hovering like he was on the toilet—and burst out laughing. He served us, no problem.   —A .V.

❏ Be a clown for the day
❏ Play the drums in pink pajamas
❏ Eat only with my hands
❏ Have a water fight in a car wash
✪ **Perform card tricks**
❏ Go dress shopping in a tutu
❏ Throw a finger-painting party
❏ Race shopping carts
❏ Sing "The Wheels on the Bus" on a bus and get everyone to join in
❏ Buy groceries wearing nothing but a trench coat and running shoes

Build a fort in your living room

You *could* meet your friends for a drink at the neighborhood bar. *Or* you could knock back cocktails in the comfort of your very own, super-deluxe living room fort! It's probably been a while since you indulged in a bit of throw-pillow and afghan architecture, so here are some tips to refresh your memory:

1. Gather tall lamps, sofas, and chairs to form the walls, arrange in a rectangle, and place the tallest piece in the center.
2. Drape a few blankets over the ensemble to fully cover three sides of the fort.
3. On the fourth side, pin the blankets back to create a doorway.
4. String up some Christmas lights, crack open a bottle of champagne, and see how many friends you can cram inside. You'll be playing truth or dare in no time.

❑ Mud wrestle
❑ Race motorized wheelchairs
✪ **Wiggle my ears**
❑ Slide down a slide backward
❑ Drop a water balloon from the top floor of a building

Be **Silly**

❑ Invent and celebrate my own holiday
❑ Play silly word games
❑ Swim in Jell-O
❑ Invent a silly walk
❑ Have a snowball fight
❑ Talk like Donald Duck
❑ Give every friend a silly nickname
✪ **Never, EVER grow up**
❑ Make a funny short film and post it on YouTube
❑ Chase butterflies and fireflies
❑ Hang upside down on a jungle gym
✪ **Start a food fight**
❑ Dress up like Cinderella
❑ Go kayaking in the rain
❑ Play hopscotch with kids I don't know
❑ Ride a Hippity-Hop
❑ Lick my elbow
❑ Bury a friend in the sand
❑ Dress up my dachshund in a hot dog costume
❑ Make funny faces at small children
❑ Cover myself in maple syrup
✪ **Wear a clown nose in public**
❑ Create silly video montages
❑ Pretend I don't speak English

- ❏ Attend the late movie in a bathrobe
- ❏ Jump in a pool full of marshmallows
- ❏ Send a singing telegram
- ❏ Play a tune on water glasses
- ❏ Get tons of food coloring and turn a public pool red
- ✪ **Leave funny messages on sugar packets in restaurants**
- ❏ Wear a giant burger costume

"I make silly bets with silly stakes."

Here are some examples:

- ■ We race to see whose elevator will make it to the eleventh floor first. Loser has to buy winner ice cream.
- ■ We guess how many Oreos we can balance on our heads. Loser has to be blindfolded and guided for a mile walk through town.
- ■ We get in different lines at the store and bet to see who will check out first.
- ■ We challenge each other to get people around us to do things or say certain things—that takes creativity!

—M. R.

- ❏ Put quarters in gumball machines and leave the gum for other people
- ❏ Eat at McDonald's in formal evening attire
- ❏ Play with a yo-yo
- ❏ Turn the city streets into a miniature golf course
- ❏ Go to a high school prom for my 30th birthday
- ❏ Paint my entire body and roll around on a canvas
- ❏ Leave messages in the condensation on car windows
- ❏ Wrestle in a kiddie pool full of chocolate pudding
- ❏ Wear a fez and drive a tiny car
- ❏ Walk into a bank wearing a bra on the outside of my clothes
- ❏ Organize a pogo stick parade

27

"Good order is the foundation of all good things." —*Edmund Burke, philosopher*

Be More Organized

Are you the kind of person who wakes up each morning thinking that today's the day you're finally going to file away those papers piling up on the kitchen table, or clean out the junk drawer(s), or pick up the dry cleaning from last winter? Do you ever wonder why you don't have anything better to worry about? Obviously, the world isn't going to fall apart if your laundry goes unfolded for a couple of days, but when clutter multiplies, it can start to feel like *everything* is out of control, like you're on a runaway train—a very crowded, messy train—that's about to derail. Creating systems to manage the everyday chaos will free up some of the energy you spend looking for your keys (and beating yourself up over losing them yet again) and let you focus on the bigger, more important stuff.

261

- ❑ Have a place for everything and keep everything in its place
- ❑ De-clutter my home
- ⚙ **Clean out my fridge**
- ❑ Organize my magazines
- ❑ Organize my knitting materials
- ❑ Spend at least 10 minutes every day tidying up
- ⚙ **Organize my e-mail**
- ❑ Make a daily to-do list that I actually follow
- ❑ Be on time

"I got rid of the stuff I didn't need."

I decided that everything I didn't use anymore HAD TO GO! I went through all my clothes and got rid of everything I hadn't worn in at least six months. From there, I took a big box that was full of CD cases and videocassettes, threw away what was ruined or I knew I would never use again, and reorganized the rest neatly in a drawer. Then I dusted the items and placed them in an orderly way. It is really hard to get rid of ALL the stuff I've been holding on to for so many years, but I've never missed anything I've thrown out. —B. B.

Create an emergency kit

Being organized beforehand is crucial during emergency situations when every minute counts. To prepare a well-stocked emergency kit, visit RedCross.org for a list of basic necessities. Make sure everyone in the family knows where the kit is kept. In addition to canned foods, bottled water, a first-aid kit, and flashlights, stock up on the following:

- Water- and windproof matches, newspaper, and other kindling materials kept dry in a ziplock bag
- Transistor or hand-crank radio and batteries
- A few hundred dollars in small bills
- Duct tape, zip ties, rope, and tools, such as pliers and a screwdriver
- Plastic sheeting such as a tarp or fiber-reinforced, laminated polyethylene film
- Copies of your passport, credit cards, and drivers license, also kept dry in a ziplock bag

❑ Update my address book
❑ Get a fireproof box for my important documents
❑ Clean up the garage and build a storage area with shelves
❑ Give away the things I don't need

- ❏ Create a weekly chore schedule
- ❏ Buy presents *before* people's birthdays and holidays
- ❏ Organize my "important papers" drawer
- ✪ **Return library books on time**
- ❏ Paint a wall-sized calendar on my wall
- ❏ Reply to e-mail in a timely manner
- ❏ Keep my house presentable for unexpected guests
- ❏ Frame my pictures

"I keep a personal recipe book."

I found an easy way to store my recipes—I use a photo album with ready-made pockets. They come in tons of different styles and fit either three-by-five or four-by-six note cards. The plastic protects your cards from liquids and dirty fingers, and the album holds a lot of cards. I keep family recipes, ones I want to try, and even ideas for cake decorating. I also take pictures of any new recipes (dorky, I know!) and then tape them to the backs. When my husband gets hungry, he pulls out the recipe book and decides what he wants for dinner. Since the recipe is right there, he can cook it himself.   —M. K.

- ❏ Clean for 5 minutes every day
- ❏ Have only useful and beautiful things in my house
- ❏ Rearrange my furniture
- ❏ Do the dishes right after dinner
- ❏ Weed my garden
- ❏ Organize my makeup and throw out anything that's more than a year old
- ❏ Create a portfolio of recent work to bring to job interviews
- ❏ Wash my sheets once a week
- ❏ Back up my computer
- ❏ Do my homework on time
- ❏ Arrange my books alphabetically by author
- ✪ **Create a system to organize my receipts and bills**
- ❏ Clean my bathroom once a week
- ❏ Organize my time better
- ❏ Dry-clean my winter coat and comforter
- ❏ Clean out my cabinets
- ❏ Buy a tie rack
- ✪ **Return phone calls**
- ❏ Reclaim the disaster formerly known as my bedroom
- ❏ Hire an accountant

Winterize the garden

Preparing gardens for a long winter nap allows soil to be replenished and dead plants to be composted. It also means you're organized and ready to begin your garden next spring.

1. Remove dead plants and toss them in compost bins. Prune perennial plants.

2. Use a pitchfork to turn over and aerate soil, and apply a four- to six-inch layer of compost.

3. Cover with six inches of shredded leaves (which you can make by running the lawn mower over a pile of leaves a couple of times). Water thoroughly.

4. After the garden has frozen, use evergreens to cover your perennial plants. (Cut up that Christmas tree!) The goal is to prevent alternate freezing and thawing. The branches hold the snow and keep it from melting or blowing away.

❑ Take care of little, picky, niggling things as they surface
❑ Find my personal organizer and start using it
❑ Clean out the fridge once a month
❑ Unsubscribe from 5 junk e-mails a day

❑ Purge and donate baby gear
❑ Put away holiday decorations in an organized manner and label the boxes
❑ Declutter my cubicle
❑ Keep my desk clean for 30 days
❑ Organize my closet by outfit, occasion, color, and season
✪ **Hire a housekeeper**
❑ Clean out my briefcase
❑ Put up storage shelves in my apartment
❑ Install new kitchen cabinets
❑ Organize the attic
❑ Write thank-you notes promptly
❑ Keep all my appointments
❑ Make a family schedule and stick to it
❑ Organize my basement and turn it into a family room
❑ Draw up a will
✪ **Consolidate my 401k accounts**
❑ Scan my important documents
❑ Consolidate all my e-mail addresses
❑ Label the recycling bins
❑ Hire out more tasks to increase my efficiency
❑ Establish an exercise routine
❑ Print out all my writing and organize it in binders

> ## "I make my bed every morning."
>
> It seems like no big deal, but if I can make the bed in the morning, I already feel like I've accomplished something. I also love coming home and having the bedroom look tidy, *and* I love getting into a bed that feels fresh every night.
>
> —S. M.

- ❏ Make time to volunteer
- ❏ Create a home office
- ❏ Set all the clocks in my house to the same time
- ❏ Break my big goals into smaller steps
- ❏ Develop a sound retirement plan
- ❏ Update my online calendar
- ❏ Clean out my bag
- ❏ Plan my days ahead of time
- ❏ Develop a habit of organization
- ❏ Go through my mail when it arrives; recycle the junk
- ❏ Winterize my home
- ✪ **Organize my DVDs**
- ❏ Clean up my computer's desktop
- ❏ Fold and put away my clothes each night

❑ Prepare a weekly menu plan

❑ Get my online bill-paying service up and running

❑ Clean out all those little drawers in the bathroom

❑ Convert my filing system from manila envelopes to hanging files

✪ **Match all the socks**

❑ Create a family bulletin board

❑ Create a monthly system of paying my bills

❑ Have a cleansing garage sale

Digitize your entire CD collection

Declutter your house and trade your bursting CD towers for a small, sleek hard drive. No more stacks of CDs getting scratched or lost. No more rummaging under your bed to find that favorite album. Whenever you're on the phone or watching TV, sit at the computer and upload CDs into your music library. Spend some time making sure the track listings and other labels are filled in correctly and are filed where you want them. Those with a music collection spanning several thousand discs should consider hiring a service such as Ready to Play (www.readytoplay.com) or Riptopia (www.riptopia.com), which will convert tunes to MP3s, organize files, and upload music to mobile devices for a fee.

28

"The minute I heard my first love
   story I started looking for you,
   not knowing how blind that
   was. Lovers don't finally meet
   somewhere. They're in each other
   all along." —*Rumi*

Find Love

People who have found love will tell you that Cupid's arrow often strikes when you least expect it. They describe it as having butterflies in your stomach, being hit by a ton of bricks, an inexplicable feeling of lightness and joy. For those who *haven't* found true love, that's not a very helpful roadmap. If you're frustrated, you're not alone. "Fall in love" and "get married" are both ranked on 43 Things' top ten all-time most popular goals. The one thing you can learn from folks who've been lucky enough to cross this one off their life list is that there's no one way to get there. They had to kiss a lot of frogs before locking eyes with their soul mate and falling in ridiculous, all-consuming, can't-live-without-each-other love—a feeling worth searching and waiting for.

- ❑ Find my Mr. Darcy
- ❑ Love without complications galore
- ❑ Go parking with my husband
- ❑ Learn how to talk to guys
- ✪ **Be someone's everything**
- ❑ Marry my high school sweetheart
- ❑ Go on one amazing first date
- ❑ Date more men
- ❑ Get a girlfriend
- ❑ Have numerous love affairs and never marry
- ❑ Tell my soul mate "yes"
- ❑ Divorce my husband and meet someone who understands me and treats me better
- ✪ **Make my wife happy**
- ❑ End my long-distance relationship by making the distance shorter
- ❑ Decide whether marriage is for me
- ❑ Be more supportive of my partner
- ❑ Get a boyfriend
- ❑ Grow old with the one I love
- ❑ Date my professor
- ❑ Deepen my relationships
- ❑ Wake up every day in someone's arms
- ❑ Seduce my husband

> ## "I fell in ridiculous, inconvenient, all-consuming, can't-live-without-each-other love."
>
> Even after nearly twenty years, he's still The One. Silly, I know. And he's such a pain in the rear. And we're so different in what we like. And I know I drive him nuts, but I can't help myself. But then I see the twinkle in his gray-blue eyes, and the boyish grin when he's done something great, and I fall in love all over again. Don't try too hard—it'll find you. It'll be like a ton of bricks fell on your head while at the same time your feet feel like you're floating on whipped cream. And when the going gets tough (and it WILL), just remember that feeling and hold on to it until the going gets better again (and it WILL). —K. M.

✪ **Get married, stay married, and live happily ever after**
❑ Start dating again
❑ Be able to love a man without having to marry him to prove my love
❑ Never go to bed angry with someone I love
❑ Date my wife
✪ **Fall in love again**

273

Learn how to flirt

Flirting can be a sales pitch to suitors, a way to interview admirers, or a coy game of getting to know each other. Here are a few ways to keep it cute the next time you approach an attractive stranger.

- Confidence is crucial, so smile, make eye contact, and remember that the worst that can happen is the person isn't interested—which is hardly the end of the world.
- Avoid canned pickup lines and initiate a casual conversation by asking open-ended questions. Or pay an easy compliment.
- Keep the chat light. Funny anecdotes are a great way to keep people interested so pull out a great story of making a fool of yourself in fifth grade. Being self-deprecating makes you seem less threatening, and reminding someone that you were once ten makes you cuter.
- Pay attention to the other person's body language. Smiles, eye contact, a light touch on the shoulder—these are all good signs. Negative body language—crossed arms, looking downward, curt answers, or a hurried demeanor—is a signal that the person isn't interested. Cut your losses and move on.

- ❑ Have a guy prove to me that they are not all the same
- ❑ Be happier in my marriage
- ❑ Understand my husband
- ✪ **Fall in love with the right person**
- ❑ Go steady
- ❑ Date somebody I wouldn't normally date
- ❑ Have at least one quiet dinner with my husband each week
- ❑ Throw a party where everyone has to bring a friend who is single

---

"I finally went on some dates."

I decided to take a major risk and join a dating website. I went on four dates, and the fourth date was the one that you could say changed my life. I wasn't necessarily standing on the edge of a cliff and this person kept me from jumping, but he restored my faith that there are good people in the world. We have been dating for two months now, and every minute with him has been fun and I've had some of the happiest days of my life. If that's what just the first two months is like, I can't wait to see what the future holds. So yes, going on a date is a great thing to do.   —S. C.

"I married my best friend."

When people say, "But he's just my best friend," I laugh.
I said that. I was totally oblivious to my true feelings for my
best friend until he confessed his own. Even then, I just felt
sorry that I couldn't offer the same feelings back. Well . . .
time progressed, and I realized that being "just friends"
was a cop-out. I allowed myself to fall head over heels in
love with the man who is now my husband (five years
coming up). If you have a best friend who makes you feel
wonderful about yourself, makes you laugh until your belly
hurts, offers the listening ear at any time, and helps you
to be the person you want to be, END the friendship and
START the romance!   —E. A.

❏ Have my family meet my fiancé's family
❏ Record a reason a day why I love my partner
   for the next 365 days
⊙ **Marry my boyfriend**
❏ Meet someone wonderful who makes me blush
   and giggle and feel fluttery, and who thinks I'm
   absolutely amazing and can't get enough of me
   . . . (and enjoy every minute of it!)
❏ Never experience a divorce

✪ **Kiss in the snow**
❑ Marry a rich man
❑ Have a long-term relationship
❑ Find a hot emo guy
❑ Be the right person instead of trying to find the right person
❑ Make my partner happy
❑ Be more understanding about my fiancé's work schedule
❑ Find a partner who will treat me as well as I deserve to be treated
❑ Understand my wife

✪ **Find true love**
❑ Meet a nice, single Jewish man
❑ Marry a rock star
❑ Ask him to divorce her
❑ Kiss for hours under a meteor shower
❑ Marry a professional baseball player
❑ Have a meaningful relationship

✪ **Love and be loved**
❑ Go to couples counseling
❑ Risk everything for love
❑ Commit to someone unconditionally . . . eventually
❑ Nurture my relationships

Try online dating

There are those who believe that the highest form of torture is making awkward conversation with a stranger over eggplant Parmesan at a mediocre Italian restaurant. But you're never going to meet the love of your life if you don't get out there. So jump into one of the following dating pools and remember, even awful dates will give you great stories with which to regale your friends.

- Sign up with It's Just Lunch (www.itsjustlunch.com). The company prescreens clients and facilitates everything from the first meeting to the follow-up.

- Join an online dating service that uses scientifically based compatibility questionnaires to make love connections between members, such as eHarmony.com, Chemistry.com, and PerfectMatch.com.

- Go on several dates in one evening by trying "speed dating." Register for events at SpeedDating.com and HurryDate.com.

❑ Find a kindred spirit
✪ **Get engaged**
❑ Meet the love of my life
❑ Find someone to share my life adventure with

❏ Take better care of my friendships

❏ Date a boy who is Wiccan

❏ Meet the right woman and have the courage to
do something about it

❏ Get a Christian girlfriend

❏ Be a worthy partner in a worthy partnership

❏ Marry for love

❏ Have an outside-in-the-rain, boom-box-overhead-
blaring "In Your Eyes" moment

✪ **Find my soul mate**

❏ Reach our 75th wedding anniversary

29

"I firmly believe that any man's finest hour, the greatest fulfillment of all that he holds dear, is that moment when he has worked his heart out in a good cause and lies exhausted on the field of battle— victorious." —*Vince Lombardi*

Compete

Add a dash of competition to your life and all
of a sudden things get a lot more interesting.
Think about it this way. What's more exciting:
a lightning-quick tennis match or practicing
your forehand solo against a wall? Your morning
jog or a 5k race? A crossword puzzle at the
kitchen table or finally filling in all the boxes
before your sister does? Competition motivates
you to push yourself harder than you would
otherwise. The thrill of throwing your hat in
the ring and proving your skills to yourself
(and anyone watching) can be physically,
mentally, and spiritually empowering. It can
also make things a lot more fun. Whether
you're trying to beat a personal best or kick
an opponent's butt, find some ways to show
the world what you're made of.

⊙ Ride in the Tour de France

❑ Enter a hula hoop contest
❑ Win a 24-hour dance marathon
❑ Enter a pie-eating contest
❑ Row competitively
❑ Letter in track
❑ Participate in the X Games
❑ Play in a golf tournament

"I completed a ride-and-tie event."*

It's been nearly a week since I completed this goal and I am still hurting! I fell off the horse during the first leg of the race and am bruised from head to toe. I ran the rest of the race with blood running down my leg and my hat full of grass and mud! The race was WAY MORE hardcore than I ever imagined it would be. The people are crazy good runners, and the horses are all amped up and would gallop the whole way if you let them. I guess because I didn't end up dying, I might actually consider trying it again (not dying—doing better in the race!).   —A. N.

*A 20- to 100-mile race where two-person teams alternate horseback riding and running across diverse terrains.

⚙ **Enter a poetry contest**
- ❏ Win the World's Strongest Man Competition
- ❏ Be a great beach volleyball player
- ❏ Be a NASCAR driver
- ❏ Win a World Series
- ❏ Compete in an obstacle course competition
- ❏ Play in a squash tournament
- ❏ Enter a facial hair competition
- ❏ Play in an NCAA football championship
- ❏ Start an extreme croquet league
- ❏ Win the Stanley Cup

⚙ **Play in the World Series of Poker**
- ❏ Win a spelling bee
- ❏ Enter a magic competition
- ❏ Win a disc golf tournament
- ❏ Race in the America's Cup
- ❏ Improve my badminton skills

⚙ **Play in the National Hockey League**
- ❏ Compete in the American Crossword Puzzle Tournament
- ❏ Join an intramural sports team
- ❏ Enter a surfing competition
- ❏ Compete in mixed martial arts
- ❏ Enter my photographs at the county fair

Host a cookies and games night

Send the following invitation to about thirty friends three weeks before your party:

In an effort to reverse the trend of decreasing board game usage in the adult population, we invite you to the first annual Cookies & Games Party. All guests should bring a batch of homemade cookies (no store-bought allowed). We'll provide milk (both cow and soy) for dunking, and if you're good, we'll mix you up a White Russian. We've got yer Jenga, Scrabble, Cranium, Monopoly, Taboo, and Scattergories, but bring a favorite game if you have one. Prizes (and penalties) to be announced.

You'll see, everyone will have more fun than when they were all eleven and spent hours and hours playing capture the flag. So dust off that Parcheesi set, sharpen your Pictionary pencil and your competitive edge, and tip those timers.

❏ Play at Wimbledon
❏ Compete in archery
❏ Play in a national bridge tournament
❏ Win an air guitar competition
❏ Breed, raise, and show a world champion horse
❏ Swim at the World Masters Games

- ❏ Participate in a figure skating competition
- ❏ Win a bicycle race
- ❏ Enter a snowboard competition
- ❏ Be a contestant on a game show
- ❏ Play in a racquetball tournament
- ❏ Win the Kentucky Derby
- ❏ Compete in a diving competition
- ✪ **Run for public office**
- ❏ Enter a salsa dance competition
- ❏ Win a karate championship
- ❏ Be on the U.S. Olympic Softball Team
- ❏ Win a trophy
- ❏ Race a Formula One car
- ❏ Become an Olympic rowing champion

"I ran the Marathon des Sables."*

The most awesome experience, physically tough and mentally shattering—you learn things about yourself that you didn't know were there and see parts of yourself that you never want to see again. Add that to being in the most amazing part of this planet and you can see why this is such a fantastic life experience.   —C. P.

*A 156-mile, six-day endurance race across Morocco's Sahara Desert held each year.

- ☐ Win the World Cup
- ☐ Play Dungeons and Dragons like I did in high school
- ☐ Win a freestyle swimming race
- ☐ Enter a competition at a local fair
- ☐ Host a badminton tournament in my backyard
- ☐ Compete in a poetry slam
- ☺ **Win a state championship**
- ☐ Enter a bodybuilding competition
- ☐ Score a touchdown
- ☐ Win the state softball championship
- ☐ Be the first female to win the X Games freestyle

Participate in a rock paper scissors tournament

At some point in childhood, you probably settled a dispute with a round of rock paper scissors. Here's your chance to raise the stakes, defeat competitors from around the world, and win thousands in prize money by competing in the annual World Rock Paper Scissors Championship. Entering requires a $40 fee, one previous sanctioned tournament, and registering at www.worldrps.com.

> ## "I completed a triathlon."
>
> I completed my first triathlon—the "summer sizzler" super sprint—this morning. Best part: pancakes, devoured afterward. Close second: the bike—big surprise! In the swim, the more I thought about going fast, the worse (and more out of breath) I became. It wasn't because I was exerting myself, just thinking about exerting myself—the weirdest experience. And then I couldn't catch my breath enough in the run to get my legs to move until almost halfway into it. But I managed to come in at exactly half of all the participants, so I can deal with that.   —R. K.

❏ Win the green jacket at the Augusta Masters
❏ Compete in a trivia tournament
❏ Enter an art contest
❏ Win a pinball tournament
❏ Enter an open-water swimming competition
✪ **Join a semiprofessional football league**
❏ Win a chess competition
❏ Challenge my brother to an arm wrestling match
❏ Be chosen most valuable player
❏ Win the Heisman Trophy
❏ Be a champion at *something*

30

"Sail away from the safe harbor. Catch the trade winds in your sails. Explore. Dream. Discover."

—*Mark Twain*

Travel More

Whether you take trips to new places or return to your favorite spots over and over again, traveling is a celebration of different cultures, customs, and cuisines and the single best way to learn about the world around you. As any seasoned globetrotter will tell you, there's more to traveling than trips to exotic locations and snapshots of assorted landmarks. Often the most treasured memories from a journey are the spontaneous side trips to out-of-the-way villages, meals at local hot spots that didn't make it into the guidebook, or getting lost in a tangle of backstreets only to spill out into a magnificent town square. A chance to see the Sistine Chapel may have been why you came to Rome, but that late-night gelato on the steps of the Trevi Fountain will be what you remember.

- ❏ Travel by myself
- ❏ Sail through the San Juan Islands
- ❏ Swim in the Neptune Pool at Hearst Castle
- ❏ See the bulls run in Pamploma
- ☺ **Drive across Canada**
- ❏ Take a fun day trip with the kids every month
- ❏ Show up at the airport with a bag and a passport and take the first available flight
- ❏ Attend the Cannes Film Festival
- ❏ Go to a hot spring
- ❏ Take a road trip making only left turns
- ❏ Go to Fashion Week in Paris
- ❏ Drive up the coast on U.S. 101
- ❏ Backpack through Europe
- ❏ See the stars on a desert island

"I floated in the Dead Sea."

You can't do much *except* float in the Dead Sea. There are so many minerals in the water that it's much denser than you are, so you bob on the surface. I tried to put my feet down straight underneath my torso, but they just popped back up. It is a very strange sensation to be in a body of water that seems to be pushing you out of it.   —C. T.

Ride the Orient Express

The Orient Express, which originated in 1883, has long been a symbol of intrigue and elite travel. Using restored rail carriages from the 1920s and 1930s, today the Venice-Simplon Orient Express (www.orient-express.com) runs a slightly modified route from Paris to Istanbul and offers the opportunity for modern-day travelers to experience the luxury, romance, and adventure of the railway immortalized in Agatha Christie's *Murder on the Orient Express* and films such as *Around the World in 80 Days*.

❏ Travel Highway 50, the Loneliest Road in America
❏ Go to New Orleans to help rebuild
✪ **Visit the Baseball Hall of Fame**
❏ Wake up to the sounds of a tropical rain forest
❏ Go on a safari
❏ Travel to exotic locations on a yacht
❏ Visit locations of Huguenot settlements
✪ **Get a passport**
❏ Take a road trip to meet my online friends
❏ Visit the Jane Goodall Institute Chimpanzee Eden in South Africa
❏ Travel off the beaten path

❑ Go on a motorcycle tour across the U.S.
❑ Float down the Boise River
❑ Visit the Hockey Hall of Fame in Toronto
❑ Take a trip down the Mekong River
✪ **See a match at Wimbledon**
❑ Go on a walkabout in Australia
❑ Take the ferry from Belfast to Stranraer
❑ Take a road trip to figure out where I want to live next
❑ Go to the World Cup
❑ Ride the train from China to Tibet
❑ Tour the wine country of South Africa
❑ Travel in a submarine
✪ **Visit every country in the world**
❑ Trek to (and then climb) Mount Everest
❑ Work for six months and travel for the other six months
❑ Visit the Georgia aquarium in Atlanta
❑ See a Broadway show
❑ Take a solo canoe trip
❑ Travel abroad with my kids
❑ Visit the countries and sites where my dad was stationed during World War II
❑ Take a 3,000-mile bicycle trip

"We took a 'one-year-off' trip."

I suspended my consulting business, my wife quit her job, and we circumnavigated the globe, visiting twenty-nine countries, taking 14,340 photos, and making nineteen new international friends. Overall, we spent $80,000 traveling and the only thing we missed about home was our dog. People often say, "I wish I could take a trip like that," and our message is that you can do it if you make the trip a priority. The key is to start planning. Set a realistic departure date and stick to it, alter your lifestyle to start saving money, and share your goal with friends and family. You'll be surprised at how things fall into place.   —L. F.

✪ **Take the ferry to Victoria, British Columbia**
❑ See the Marfa Mystery Lights in Texas
❑ Revisit all the places I've lived
❑ Take a road trip after graduation
❑ Visit every preserved ancient civilization in the world
❑ Drive I-40 all the way to the ocean
❑ Visit the El Rosario Monarch Butterfly Sanctuary in Mexico
❑ Go to Tokyo

- ❏ Take a road trip to towns with weird names
- ✪ **Go on a safari in West Africa**
- ❏ Ride horseback through Ireland
- ❏ Go to the Rose Bowl
- ❏ Drive all night and see where I end up
- ❏ Ride all the Melbourne tram routes to the end of the line
- ❏ Visit the major art museums of the world
- ❏ Sail a boat to Mexico
- ❏ Take a long train trip through the Rockies
- ❏ Go to the Sapporo Snow Festival in Japan
- ❏ Visit the lands of my ancestors
- ✪ **Climb to the top of the Eiffel Tower**
- ❏ Visit every lighthouse in America
- ❏ Play with penguins at the South Pole
- ❏ Sail across the Atlantic Ocean
- ❏ Ride a camel across the Sahara Desert
- ❏ Visit the Western Wall in Jerusalem
- ❏ Take a motorcycle trip to Alaska
- ❏ Visit every capital city in the world
- ❏ Meditate at Stonehenge
- ❏ Visit the Amsterdam Red Light District
- ❏ Take a road trip through Texas for the barbecue

Join an Earthwatch expedition

Visit exotic locations, work alongside scientists, and help preserve disappearing cultures and the environment by volunteering with the Earthwatch Institute, a nonprofit organization that performs conservation work and research around the world. Spend your vacation helping archaeologists excavate an eleventh-century castle of Catignano in Tuscany or monitor the sea life in and around Thailand's coral reefs. Volunteers are placed with a team of experts ranging in size from four to twelve people, provided with meals and accommodations, and trained on-site. Join an expedition at www.earthwatch.org.

❏ Explore Mayan ruins in Mexico
❏ Have dinner at the Moulin Rouge
✪ **Drive across the United States**
❏ Visit every James Bond film location
❏ Light a candle in the United States Holocaust Memorial Museum's Hall of Rememberance
❏ Travel the Silk Road in Asia
❏ Drink wine and people-watch at a sidewalk café in Paris
❏ Go on an archaeological dig

"I traveled on a freighter."

Traveling by freighter was one of my coolest travel experiences. The ship quarters were comfortable and I had my own shower and a couch, desk, single bed, and small window through which I could see the wake of the ship. Simple but solid meals were served in the mess room three times a day. The company on the ship was diverse—German and Polish officers, a Filipino crew, and a few other oddball passengers like me: two Swedes traveling around the world without flying, a retired embalmer and his wife from Brisbane, a mother and daughter who were afraid to fly, and me on my big adventure to see the world. At night, most of the crew and passengers congregated in the officers' room to drink, play cards, and tell stories as only seamen can.

As we passed countless tropical islands in Indonesia, the water was so clear you could see the sand welling up on the ocean floor. I spent my days reading, talking, and hanging around the bridge observing, asking questions, and tracking our progress on maps and a GPS system. The vibrations from the engines, the gentle roll of the ship, tropical sun, and breathtaking sights are something that I'll remember for the rest of my life.

— K. A.

❏ Visit an ashram
❏ Retrace Che Guevera's motorcycle trip through South America
❏ Visit a monastery
❏ Take a trip with my mom
❏ Go to Venice and ride in a gondola

⊕ **Travel to Mecca**

❏ Ride the Red River Canyon train in Mexico
❏ Explore old movie locations
❏ Go to Mass in Vatican City
❏ Visit the Rock and Roll Hall of Fame
❏ Rent a villa in Florence for a year

⊕ **Stay at the Ice Hotel in Iceland**

❏ Throw a dart into a map and travel to wherever it lands
❏ Light a candle for peace at Westminster Abbey
❏ Go to a rock concert on Mount Fuji in Japan
❏ Visit the Vietnam Memorial in Washington, D.C.
❏ Take an overnight horseback trip in the Grand Teton mountains
❏ Ride a steamboat down the Mississippi River
❏ Attend the Burning Man festival
❏ Take a surf trip to Baja
❏ Tour World War II battlefields in Europe

See the (new) Seven Wonders of the World

Fires, earthquakes, and wars destroyed all but one of the original Seven Wonders of the World, the Great Pyramid of Giza. But in 2007, in an initiative led by a Swiss-based foundation, 10 million people voted and revised the list. You may not agree with all the choices, but the following places are certainly worth a visit:

- **The Great Wall of China** is more than 4,160 miles long and was built in the fifth century to prevent Mongolian tribes from invading.
- **Christ the Redeemer Statue,** a 130-foot-tall, 700-ton concrete figure of Jesus with open arms, towers over Rio de Janeiro from its perch on Mount Corcovado.
- **The 50,000-seat Roman Colosseum** was the largest amphitheater ever built in the Roman Empire and

❏ Visit all the colleges at Oxford University
✪ **Follow a band on tour**
❏ Explore a jungle
❏ Backpack around the world
❏ Eat sushi in Japan
❏ Take a trip on a Goodyear blimp

notoriously hosted gladiatorial contests and other events for almost 500 years.

- **Machu Picchu,** an Incan village nestled on the side of a mountaintop in the Peruvian rainforest, was forgotten for centuries and rediscovered in 1911.
- **Chichen Itza,** a grand temple and city on Mexico's Yucatan Peninsula, served as the political and economic center of the ancient Mayan civilization.
- **The Taj Mahal** in Agra, India, is a luminous white domed marble-and-tile mausoleum built by Mughal emperor Shah Jahan as a tribute to his favorite wife.
- **Petra,** an ancient city carved directly into the red rock mountains forming the eastern flank of the Arabah in Jordan, boasts examples of advanced architecture, including water chambers and a 4,000-seat theater.

❏ Zipline over the Amazon
❏ Go camping in Big Sur
❏ Sail the Mediterranean
❏ Go shopping on the Champs-Élysées
❏ Visit the Forbidden City in Beijing
❏ Take a motorcycle trip through South America

✪ Circumnavigate the globe
☐ See the world's most spectacular waterfalls
☐ Be in New York for the Macy's Thanksgiving Day Parade
☐ Ride the Chunnel train from England to France
☐ Take a bike tour of Italy's wine country
☐ Visit every Formula One race track
☐ See a rugby match in London

✪ Go to the Olympic Games
☐ Visit an orphanage in Uganda
☐ Celebrate Cinco de Mayo in Mexico
☐ Visit Mount Rushmore
☐ Take a trip to Churchill, Canada, to see the polar bears
☐ Visit Dracula's castle in Transylvania
☐ Take a mother, daughters, and granddaughter trip
☐ Visit the Crazy Horse Memorial in South Dakota
☐ Take a canoe trip along the Lewis and Clark route
☐ Ride every Washington state ferry at least once

❑ Ride a Vespa through the streets of Rome

❑ Explore the pyramids of Egypt

❑ Visit Taganyika Wildlife Park in Africa

⊙ **Attend the Sundance Film Festival**

❑ Take a bicycle trip through Holland

❑ Party in Paris on Bastille Day

❑ Samba at Carnival in Brazil

❑ Visit a different Civil War battlefield each year

❑ Go see a NASA shuttle launch

❑ Do yoga in India

❑ Take my sons on a "fly-in" fishing trip to Canada

❑ Visit a winery in Napa Valley

❑ Go to Cancun for spring break

❑ Explore the routes of the Underground Railroad

❑ Revisit the place where I met my spouse

⊙ **Visit Disneyland**

❑ Take a girls-only trip to Vegas

❑ Travel across Ireland, staying in hostels

❑ Take a houseboat trip through the canals
   in France

31

"Human beings are not born once and for all on the day their mothers give birth to them, but life obliges them over and over again to give birth to themselves."

—*Gabriel Garcia Márquez*

Reinvent Myself

Ever wish you could just wipe the slate clean, hit restart, and try again? Well, you're not a blackboard and you can't travel back in time, but starting over is within your grasp. Sometimes what you need is a big change—a new career, a different city, a fresh relationship. Other times seemingly superficial changes like a new wardrobe or a new haircut can be enough to refresh your spirit. A new you in one area of your life can give you the momentum you need to change other areas (and remind you that you're in control). So whenever you fall into a rut, stumble on hard times, or need to bounce back from a less-than-perfect year, remember that reinvention, especially when you're the one calling the shots, is never a bad thing.

❑ Become the person I've always wanted to be
❑ Dye my hair red
❑ Get a new job in a new city
❑ Get a boob job
❑ Have corrective jaw surgery
❑ Don't be so naive
❑ Become stronger, more courageous, more daring, more relentless
✪ **Redecorate my apartment**
❑ Develop a daily self-improvement program
❑ Grow out my bangs
❑ Have a totally different life by this time next year

"I changed directions."

My first step was to think about what I wanted to be and where I wanted to go as a person. For me, it involved doing anything with my law school degree but practicing law. (I can still hear my father and mother wailing *Noooo*!!!) In order to do this, you need to realize that you can and do impact your own life. Ask yourself what steps you can take to make a change. Then do it. Enough small things change in your life and you have changed yourself. —K. R.

❏ Get corrective eye surgery
❏ Be absurdly classy
❏ Have clear skin
✪ **Shave my head**
❏ Get colored contacts
❏ Be more talkative
❏ Break off my engagement
❏ Get dreadlocks
❏ Whiten my teeth
❏ Get new glasses
❏ Wear skirts more often
❏ Let my hair go gray and add silver accents
❏ Get a face-lift
❏ Be more feminine
❏ Change my annoying laugh
❏ Update my wardrobe
❏ Get liposuction
❏ Develop a thick skin
❏ Become more of a free spirit
✪ **Have an open mind**
❏ Lose my accent
❏ Gain 10 pounds
❏ Come out of the closet
❏ Tone my body

✪ **Move to another country**
- ❏ Grow a mustache
- ❏ Change my tattoo
- ❏ Become more sophisticated
- ❏ Get a nose job
- ❏ Have gastric bypass surgery
- ❏ Wear all black for a week
- ❏ Grow a beard
- ❏ Downsize my life
- ❏ Switch careers
- ❏ Be seductive

✪ **Get my tongue pierced**
- ❏ Practice good etiquette

Cut off all of your hair for a cause

Shedding your mane is as close as you can come to shedding a piece of yourself, and it's a quick and relatively affordable way to be ceremoniously reborn. Simultaneously change your own life and brighten someone else's by sending your discarded tresses to Locks of Love (www.locksoflove.org), which uses donated hair to create hairpieces for children fighting long-term diseases or undergoing treatments that result in baldness.

"I want to make a big change."

In order to make a big change in your life, first you must *want* to change. This is different from feeling like you ought to change or wishing you could change. Next, make yourself aware of the ways you sabotage yourself or block your own progress. Third, be a patient, benevolent parent to yourself. You'll make mistakes—it's good to know that in advance— but gently guide yourself back with love and do what you can to set the ideal conditions for your success.   — P. Y.

❑ Start wearing makeup
❑ Create a personal growth journal
⊙ **Look good in a bikini**
❑ Be the kind of person people naturally respect and admire
❑ Take voice lessons to get a deeper voice
❑ Create a list of values that I admire and begin to embody them
❑ Start wearing suits
❑ Be more mysterious
❑ Wax my eyebrows
❑ Live a more bohemian lifestyle
❑ Be less ditzy

Change your name

As long as you're not changing your name to do something shady like escape creditors, the government doesn't have much problem granting your request. The process involves a lot of paperwork and varies slightly from state to state, but in general here's what you can expect:

1. Obtain forms from your city or county registrar's office or USlegalforms.com. They include a petition for change of name, an order granting the name, a legal backer form, a notice of petition to the public, an affidavit of consent, and an affidavit of service of notification.

2. Fill out the forms and have them notarized. Submit the paperwork and wait for approval of your name. (This may require going before a judge.)

3. Place an advertisement in the local newspaper announcing your new name. (This is a funny quirk of the law—it's called "a notice of petition to the public.")

4. Use the granting order to apply for a new driver's license, Social Security card, and new birth certificate at your state's Bureau of Records and Vital Statistics.

Still want to change your name?

- ❏ Change my gender
- ❏ Have a kick-ass body that stops traffic
- ❏ Defy stereotypes
- ❏ Straighten my hair
- ✪ **Pierce my nose**
- ❏ Go a week without wearing makeup
- ❏ Become an intellectual
- ❏ Be a punk
- ❏ Phase the color pink out of my wardrobe
- ❏ Develop a distinguished alter ego
- ❏ Grow my hair really long
- ❏ Be more dashing

"I got my teeth fixed."

I had severe overcrowding and my canine tooth on the right side overlapped, so in high school people said I looked like a vampire. I felt so embarrassed to open my mouth that I smiled with my mouth closed. I don't know why it took me so long, but I finally made the decision to get braces when I was twenty-seven. It was a bit weird to have braces as an adult, but not too bad. People tell me I seem more confident now when I talk and smile, and it's true.   — R. T.

32

"Faith is taking the first step even when you don't see the whole staircase." —*Martin Luther King Jr.*

Have Faith

At certain points in your life, often after a crisis or a life-changing event, you're forced to confront the big questions. Loss leads to a reflection on the meaning of life. Changes in your job can trigger larger uncertainties about your future. Criticism from a friend has you wondering if you really *are* a good person. When you feel adrift, faith can be what pulls you back to your center. Faith can provide comfort and a set of guidelines for living, but ultimately faith is a source of strength. It helps you do what's right even when it's really difficult. Discover what nourishes your soul by stripping away externals like material goods and listening to that little voice inside your head. In defining your beliefs and putting them into practice, you'll develop a spiritual compass to chart your life's course.

- ❑ Pray out loud daily
- ⚙ **Preach the gospel**
- ❑ Live my beliefs
- ❑ Make a list of the prayers God has answered
- ❑ Repent
- ❑ Create my own destiny
- ❑ Believe good things happen to good people
- ❑ Find a religion that fits my beliefs
- ❑ Join a Bible study group
- ❑ Believe in a higher power
- ❑ Develop my own ethical code
- ❑ Live by the Ten Commandments
- ❑ Be born-again
- ❑ Practice Wicca
- ❑ Believe in something
- ❑ Study the Kabbalah
- ❑ Be a better example of my faith

"I look for God everywhere."

You find Him in the weirdest of places. Sometimes not in churches, temples, mosques, or synagogues, but rather in the woods, the mountains, in someone's eyes, in someone's heart, and maybe just maybe, in your own heart.   —S. E.

Explore different faiths

Educate yourself about Buddhism, Islam, Christianity, or any faith that sparks your interest by visiting a different church, temple, or mosque each week and participating in religious services. Or take the spiritual survey at Beliefnet.com and answer questions about such things as the existence of a higher power, origins of the universe, the afterlife, and social values. The site will tally your responses and match your personal beliefs with religious faiths. Launch your spiritual explorations from there.

❑ Never, ever give up hope
❑ Have regular scripture study
❑ Officially become a member of my church
❑ Believe in serendipity
❑ Achieve enlightenment
❑ Develop a spiritual life
❑ Try voodoo
✪ **Read the Quran on a daily basis and contemplate its meaning**
❑ Take a leap of faith
❑ Participate more in my church
❑ Serve the Lord

Go on a walking meditation

In contrast to a sitting meditation, a walking meditation establishes a mind-body connection while you're in motion and have your eyes open. Wildmind.org, an online resource for Buddhist mediation, has an excellent guide that takes you through a walking meditation. Here it is in its simplest form:

1. Stand very still, take a few slow, deep breaths, and feel your body's weight equally distributed in both feet.

2. Start walking at a slow, easy pace. Feel your foot muscles release and contract with each step you take.

3. As you walk, move your awareness from your feet to focus on the ankle joints and tendons. Then move your attention through your lower legs, upper legs, pelvic area, abdomen, and chest, and consciously relax each area.

4. Notice any feelings such as the absence or presence of pain, emotions, and thoughts. Just notice, don't react.

5. When you come to a stop, take note of how it feels to no longer be moving, feel again your body's weight through the soles of your feet, and bring the meditation to a close.

❏ Attend temple at least once a month
❏ Discover God or discover that there is no God
❏ Practice Buddhism
❏ Become active in the Lutheran church
❏ Resist temptation
❏ Spend more time with God
❏ Be more spiritual without being spooky
❏ Become a nun
❏ Pray with more focus
❏ Have a spiritual awakening
❏ Light a candle in a Buddhist temple
❏ Define my faith
❏ Relocate my lost spirituality
❏ Act as I believe
❏ Recognize God's voice
❏ Believe the unbelievable
❏ Forgive God
❏ Have unshakable faith
✪ **Create my own religion**
❏ Get in touch with my spiritual side
❏ Maintain my faith through good and bad times
❏ Be proud of my faith
❏ Become a priest
❏ Convert to another religion

"I found a church that works for me."

I recently started going to a well-established nondenominational church and I walk out of the church every Sunday with such a different and wonderful outlook on the day—and on life in general. I'm a firm believer in experiencing many different churches until you find the one for you. That's exactly what it took for me, and now I feel like I am at home.   —S. E.

- ❏ Have faith that there is life after death
- ❏ Pray regularly and wholeheartedly
- ❏ Strengthen my spiritual beliefs
- ❏ Renew my faith in God
- ❏ Be a prayer warrior
- ❏ Attend a service of another religion
- ❏ Have the faith I once had as a child
- ❏ Believe in fate
- ❏ Be committed to my faith
- ✪ **Be more patient**
- ❏ Explore my faith
- ❏ Improve my spiritual life
- ❏ Trust God

- ❏ Go to confession
- ❏ Show the world the good in Islam and Muslims
- ❏ Have coffee time with God daily
- ❏ Renew my Catholic faith
- ✪ **Have faith in myself**
- ❏ Devote my life to God
- ❏ Find a spiritual community
- ❏ Deepen my faith
- ❏ Know if my relationship with God is real
- ❏ Have faith that everything will be OK
- ❏ Never lose faith
- ❏ Give my priest a real confession (for a change)
- ❏ Have faith that the universe will provide

Build an altar

Create a sacred space for prayer and reflection or to honor ancestors and loved ones. Find a nook or corner in your house that's slightly out of the way. Your altar can be as elaborate or as simple as you like. Consider getting a small table, stool, or bench covered with some fabric on which to place candles and incense. Decorate with photos, flowers, a prayer book, and inspiring images or symbols. Surround yourself with things that bring you peace and focus.

"I found a way to be spiritual without religion."

I was and am an atheist, but I discovered how important spirituality is and how it works in my life. I ignored my negative feelings about organized religion and saw how people maintained relationships with whatever their higher power was. I saw how things worked for them, came up with parallels that worked in my life, and found a daily spiritual pursuit that works for me. I definitely feel the difference. I have more peace, serenity, joy, happiness, enthusiasm, drive, motivation, and fulfillment in my life than I ever had before. It's a wonderful way to live. —A.S.P.

✪ Believe in God
❑ Go on a spiritual retreat
❑ Practice my faith, not my religion
❑ Go to seminary
❑ Discover the meaning of faith
❑ Reconnect with my religion
❑ Accomplish what God sent me here to do
❑ Believe in the good in people
❑ Learn about religions—even if I'm not religious

❏ Go on a retreat to a monastery

❏ Hold on to my faith

✪ **Study the Torah**

❏ Get closer to God

❏ Understand Islam

❏ Give something up for Lent and stick with it

❏ Give Christianity a second chance

❏ Find faith in love

❏ Embrace my spiritual side

❏ Remember to love all God's creatures

❏ Have a stronger faith . . . heck, have faith in
something, period

33

"... Dance while you can,
Dance, dance for the figure is easy,
The tune is catching and will
   not stop;
Dance till the stars come down
   from the rafters;
Dance, dance, dance till you drop."

—*W. H. Auden*

Dance!

Dancing is a miracle drug. Whether it's the waltz or the Macarena, dancing releases mood-enhancing endorphins and transports you to a blissful state where inhibitions vanish and spirits lift. Anger dissipates while grooving to your favorite band, self-consciousness melts away in an undulating crowd at a dance club, and you'll feel lighter than air as you float across the ballroom floor. So take a cue from Napoleon Dynamite and wow a crowd with a choreographed number, learn the steps to the finale of Michael Jackson's "Thriller," or sign up for a Lindy Hop class. Whenever the going gets tough, get out on the dance floor and get your groove on—even if it's just in the privacy of your own living room with the stereo blaring.

- ❑ Dance when there is no music
- ❑ Ballroom dance at a fancy party
- ❑ Slow dance in a parking lot
- ❑ Dance like Fred Astaire
- ✪ **Dance with my wife**
- ❑ Dance down a supermarket aisle
- ❑ Boogie oogie oogie till I just can't boogie no more
- ❑ Dance in a music video
- ❑ Give myself permission to bust a move
- ✪ **Dance like Michael Jackson**
- ❑ Dance with a stranger in a strange land
- ❑ Break out into spontaneous dancing in public like they do in the musicals

"I dance to let it all out."

Dancing is such an emotional release for me. Whenever I'm feeling a little blue or stressed, I grab my girlfriends and we shake it like there's no tomorrow. When I dance, I don't worry about the person next to me. Dancing is nothing more than moving with confidence—you don't have to have any formal training to have a great time. At the end of the night, I guarantee you'll feel like a million bucks—I always do. —S. Y.

Dance the Viennese waltz in Vienna

Couples dressed in extravagant evening wear floating through chandeliered ballrooms, gracefully dancing in circles, might seem like the stuff of fairy tales. But you can actually attend balls worthy of Cinderella and her prince in the Austrian capital of Vienna, which hosts hundreds of such events during a three-month season starting November 11. Dancing at one of these balls requires proficiency in the Viennese waltz, the classic and oldest ballroom-dance style, dating back to the late 1700s. (It was considered quite risqué at the time because partners had to hold each other so closely.) The Viennese waltz is four times faster than the American waltz, so consider taking lessons at a local studio; or if you have some dance experience, go to BallroomDancers.com for descriptions of the steps and practice on your own. Then check the ball calendar (www.ballkalender.info), book your flight, and get ready to twirl all night.

❑ Dance to folk music in an Irish pub
❑ Dance in the streets
❑ Tap dance for change on a New York street corner
❑ Dance all night

Be a better dance partner

Most dancing these days doesn't involve the standard lead-follow relationship. But the next time someone asks you to dance (whether at a club or a formal soiree), be a confident partner and keep these tips in mind.

- Don't be afraid to make eye contact. Connecting with your partner is the only way you're going to, quite literally, anticipate your partner's next moves.
- Be receptive and have a gentle touch. No one likes a bossy dance partner.
- Be mindful of the other person's shape—make sure their arms are at a comfortable height and find a stride or swivel that works for both of you.
- Don't overthink it! Listen to the beat of the music and enjoy yourself.

❑ Dance every day of my life
❑ Compete in a swing-dance competition
❑ Dance from one end of a subway car to the other
❑ Attend a Lindy Hop dance in Scotland
✪ **Be a ballerina**
❑ Dance at a Cajun festival

Dance!

❑ Go to a real square dance, barn included

✪ **Learn how to dance to hip-hop**

❑ Dance on the table at a party

❑ Dance and laugh with my kids

❑ Dance with glee

❑ Do the robot dance extremely awesomely

❑ Dance with my father at my wedding

❑ Dance on the side of a mountain

❑ Learn merengue

❑ Dance around in my underwear

❑ Dance the tango in Buenos Aires

❑ Dance for my sanity

❑ Go to an underground salsa club

✪ **Join a dance squad**

❑ Dance professionally at least once in my life

❑ Become a burlesque dancer

"I danced in the moonlight."

Last summer I went to the lake with my friends. The moon was so full and bright; it felt like the sun, only more subtle, cool, and calm. I wandered off by myself, over the hill. I whirled around, spun, and it felt so nice—like my soul had been aching to do it for years.　　　—C. P.

- ❏ Go disco dancing
- ❏ Be able to dance at age 100
- ❏ Dance in a graveyard
- ✪ **Break dance**
- ❏ Silly dance all around my building
- ❏ Dance like John Travolta
- ❏ Choreograph a Broadway musical
- ❏ Dance the Charleston in a champagne fountain
- ❏ Slam dance
- ❏ Dance in roller skates
- ❏ Find my rhythm
- ❏ Dirty dance
- ❏ Dance on a rooftop under a full moon
- ❏ Whistle and dance on a Parisian night
- ✪ **Learn to country line dance**
- ❏ Do the chicken dance
- ❏ Dance down a boardwalk
- ❏ Dance in *The Nutcracker*
- ❏ Dance under a waterfall
- ❏ Do the polka
- ❏ Dance the hora at my wedding
- ❏ Ask my crush to dance
- ❏ Dance and sing in the shower

- ❑ Dance with my dog
- ❑ Find the perfect dance partner
- ✪ **Dance like Ginger Rogers**
- ❑ Win a dance-off
- ❑ Learn to dance to the beat
- ❑ Dance in the dark
- ❑ Go to a rave
- ❑ Dance a jig out of pure excitement
- ❑ Learn how to fox-trot
- ❑ Lead a conga line

Eighteen of the best dance movies ever

Watch these movies with the volume turned up anytime you want, or need, a reason to shake it.

- *Chicago* (2002)
- *Dirty Dancing* (1987)
- *Fame* (1980)
- *Flashdance* (1983)
- *Footloose* (1984)
- *Hair* (1979)
- *High School Musical* (2006)
- *Mad Hot Ballroom* (2005)
- *Napoleon Dynamite* (2004)
- *Rize* (2005)
- *Saturday Night Fever* (1977)
- *Shall We Dance?* (1996)
- *Singin' in the Rain* (1952)
- *Strictly Ballroom* (1992)
- *The Full Monty* (1997)
- *The Tango Lesson* (1997)
- *Top Hat* (1935)
- *West Side Story* (1961)

"I hosted a wild dance party in my bedroom."

I threw an incredible bedroom dance party—totally spur of the moment and completely amazing. The key is to get as many people into one room as possible and make it so fun that they'll never want to stop dancing. No big-time stereo necessary—I just used $30 speakers hooked up to my computer and the party didn't suffer one bit —in fact, it helped, because folks could search for tunes they wanted to hear and dance out even harder.   —M. B.

❑ Ballroom dance at my senior prom
✪ **Dance on Broadway**
❑ Dance the flamenco with a very
   beautiful girl
❑ Be a graceful hula dancer
❑ Do a perfect triple pirouette
❑ Do an interpretive dance in public
❑ Dance down the Sunset Strip
❑ Dance without having to be drunk
❑ Take a dance class with my daughter
❑ Take an exotic dance class
❑ Dance till dawn in a Spanish nightclub

Dance!

- ❏ Dance in the kitchen with the man of my dreams
- ✪ **Learn how to dance in a club**
- ❏ Dance under the stars
- ❏ Dance with a scarf
- ✪ **Dance on the beach**
- ❏ Dance with knives
- ❏ Take an African dance class
- ❏ Really, really learn ballet
- ❏ Dance in the mud
- ❏ Dance with a professional dance company
- ❏ Dance in a cage
- ❏ Dance *en pointe*
- ❏ Teach someone to dance
- ❏ Dance with a monkey
- ❏ Learn to dance something other than a slow dance
- ❏ Dance with the devil in the pale moonlight
- ❏ Dance at a wedding reception
- ✪ **Learn ballroom dancing**
- ❏ Learn how to bump and grind
- ❏ Dance on the clouds

34

"When we heal the earth,
we heal ourselves."

—David Orr, environmentalist

Save the Planet

It's easier than ever to tread lightly on the planet, so there is no longer any excuse for living at the earth's expense. Every decision, or nondecision, you make about what to buy, eat, or discard either harms or helps the environment. Become conscious of your daily routine, take a look at sustainable ways to consume, and curb wasteful habits. Even small changes can have a big impact. Once you raise your own awareness and refuse, for example, to use plastic bags, it's just one step to lobbying city hall to ban plastic bags in your town. Such simple changes in your habits set a tone for the future, lay a foundation for bigger improvements, and ensure that tomorrow will be a little better than yesterday.

✪ **Carpool to work**
❑ Practice mindful consumption
❑ Recycle more
❑ Use public transportation for a year
❑ Eat more locally grown food
❑ Buy a bike
❑ Grow an herb garden
✪ **Buy eco-friendly products**
❑ Use natural beauty products
❑ Take a biointensive gardening course
❑ Implement a recycling program at my office
❑ Run my dishwasher only with a full load
❑ Build a solar house
❑ Install a gray water system in my house
✪ **Use cloth diapers**

"I use cloth grocery bags."

I think the key for me was to get a good cloth bag that folded up really small, so I could just stuff it into any handbag that I took out with me. Saves the environment, lets me feel good about myself, and allows the promotion of individuality, all in one little goal!   —N. F.

Buy organic cotton

Farming traditional cotton provides about half of the world's fiber needs (and probably half of your wardrobe), but it also involves more chemicals per unit than any other crop. According to the World Wildlife Fund, cotton farming accounts for 11 percent of agricultural chemical use and 24 percent of the sale of insecticides. Just growing enough cotton for a T-shirt requires a third of a pound of chemicals, which isn't healthy for you or the planet. Unlike conventional cotton, organic cotton is farmed without pesticides, herbicides, insecticides, or other chemicals. Who would have thought that overhauling your underwear drawer could reduce your environmental impact?

❏ Turn down the thermostat at night and when I am not going to be home
❏ Always turn off the lights when I leave a room
❏ Eat only sustainable fish
❏ Pick up trash off the streets and dispose of it properly
❏ Cut down on my light pollution
✪ **Never accept a plastic bag**
❏ Buy an energy-efficient kettle

Get an energy audit

Expose areas where energy is being lost, check the
efficiency of your furnace and air-conditioning, and find ways
to conserve hot water and electricity with an energy audit.
To conduct your own audit, follow these tips:

1. Shut exterior doors, windows, and fireplace flues, turn off
   gas-burning furnaces and other combustion appliances,
   and start exhaust fans (if you have them) to remove air
   from rooms. Use a wet hand or smoking incense to detect
   leaks around baseboards, attic hatches, window frames,
   and other areas. Plug or caulk any leaks.

2. Take samples of insulation from the attic and walls
   and consult the U.S. Department of Energy's online
   Insulation Fact Sheet to assess if the type of insulation
   is sufficient.

3. Check and change heating and cooling equipment filters,
   replace systems more than fifteen years old, and have
   units professionally cleaned once a year.

4. Swap out high-wattage lightbulbs with 60-watt bulbs,
   and consider installing compact fluorescent lightbulbs
   in rooms with high usage.

Learn more about conserving at www.eere.energy.gov.

- ❏ Make biodiesel the standard fuel
- ❏ Turn off my computer when I'm not using it
- ❏ Get a rain barrel to help conserve water
- ❏ Save and reuse bows and ribbons from gifts
  I receive
- ❏ Build a strong, environmentally conscious business
- ✪ **Plant bamboo**
- ❏ Strive to wear only natural-fiber clothing
- ❏ Make the world aware of alternative pest control
- ❏ Use reusable cloth napkins
- ✪ **Buy carbon offsets**
- ❏ Start a nontoxic housecleaning company
- ❏ Switch to energy-efficient lightbulbs
- ✪ **Live off the grid**

"I bike to work."

I'm a bike commuter and I love it. You can save the environment literally tons (yes, thousands of pounds) of greenhouse emissions per year all while getting fit. You'll feel free—not relying on gas, not dealing with lame traffic—and you'll experience the journey at a more intimate level (in the open air with the birds and other critters). Enjoy your bike and make it part of your lifestyle.   —C. N.

"I grow my own food."

Nothing's better than a fresh tomato, cucumber, or watermelon right out of the garden. Heck, sometimes it doesn't even make it out of the garden! What we don't eat goes to friends, family, coworkers, or our animals. No chemical fertilizer, just manure from our animals, which is a wonderful circle to be a part of. Grow something! Even if it's just a tomato or pepper plant in an old coffee can.   —R. T.

- ❑ Design an eco-friendly yacht
- ❑ Educate the public on climate change
- ❑ Teach business in a way that inspires ethical, sustainable action
- ❑ Replace Tupperware with glass Pyrex dishes
- ❑ Advocate for renewable energy
- ❑ Become less reliant on oil
- ✪ **Buy an electric bike**
- ❑ Use wind power for my home
- ❑ Support conservationism
- ❑ Consume less paper
- ❑ Advocate for more greenways and parks in my city
- ❑ Build a solar water heater

❑ Ban incandescent lightbulbs in the United States

✪ **No more styrofoam cups!**

❑ Use plastic sandwich bags as little as possible

❑ Reuse wrapping paper at least once

❑ Commercialize the production of used cooking oil as fuel

❑ Use rags instead of paper towels

❑ Install a rainwater recycling system

✪ **Have my own sustainable farm**

❑ Be an environmental activist

❑ Practice mindful disposal

❑ Recycle my batteries

❑ Discover high-quality, eco-friendly makeup

❑ Plant more seedlings

❑ Take shorter showers

✪ **Drive a solar-electric car**

❑ Get my apartment complex to recycle

❑ Open an organic, eco-friendly restaurant

❑ Replace all my windows with double-pane energy-efficient windows

❑ Host a symposium on sustainable communities

❑ Recycle old school books

❑ Get energy-efficient appliances

❑ Install a green roof

Have a green wedding

Even if you're going all out on your big day, there are several ways—large and small—to protect the planet while tying the knot.

- Print invitations with soy ink on recycled paper.
- Ask caterers to use local or organic food and wine.
- Decorate with potted plants or local, in-season flowers.
- Choose rings made from conflict-free diamonds from retailers such as Brilliant Earth (www.brilliantearth.com) or vintage wedding bands from Green Karat (www.greenkarat.com).
- Plant a tree in each guest's name instead of giving favors.

Find more ideas at Green Elegance Weddings (www.greeneleganceweddings.com) and Portovert (www.portovert.com)

- ❑ Dispose of garbage in biodegradable bags
- ❑ Recycle my old cell phones
- ❑ Fill my apartment with air-purifying plants
- ❑ Drive a fuel-efficient car
- ❑ Be an eco-friendly fashion designer

☐ Recycle all my plastic water and soda bottles
⊙ **Conserve natural resources**
☐ Sign up for a car-share program
☐ Don't let the water run when brushing my teeth
☐ Run my car on ethanol
⊙ **Plant flowers**
☐ Get my parents to recycle
☐ Support Greenpeace
☐ Lobby for environmental legislation
☐ Recycle my old computer
☐ Insulate my attic
☐ Stop buying things tested on animals
☐ Plant a rooftop garden
⊙ **Drive a hybrid car**
☐ Use it up, wear it out, make it do, or do without

35

"When you can do the common things of life in an uncommon way, you will command the attention of the world." —*Thomas Carlyle, writer*

Be **Famous**

Celebrities may lament the hassles of living in a fishbowl, but they can't tarnish the allure of stardom for the rest of us. For some, fame delivers the ultimate validation: recognition of your talents, public admiration—not to mention glitz and glamour. Andy Warhol's theory, "In the future, everyone will be world-famous for fifteen minutes" may have been prophetic. Becoming famous isn't so difficult these days, now that reality TV shows and YouTube videos have transformed hundreds of regular folks into household names. Of course, there are still those with loads of talent and a strong work ethic who become famous the old-fashioned way. Whatever way you do it, stepping into the spotlight is about being brave enough to think you deserve it. So stop waiting to be discovered. The clock is ticking on your fifteen minutes.

- ❏ Get a star on the Hollywood Walk of Fame
- ❏ Be cast in a TV pilot
- ❏ Become a Pulitzer Prize–winning author
- ❏ Be *People* magazine's Sexiest Man Alive
- ❏ Have an article written about me
- ❏ Exhibit my photographs at the Museum of Modern Art
- ❏ Make a movie that goes down in history
- ❂ **Win a Grammy**
- ❏ Be acknowledged for my lifetime achievements
- ❏ Have a disease named after me
- ❏ Invent something that will change the world
- ❏ Be famous for doing nothing
- ❏ Lead a social revolution
- ❏ Be known only by my first name
- ❏ Win an Apple Design Award
- ❏ Be remembered by history
- ❏ Have a scholarship named in my honor
- ❏ Own a media empire
- ❏ Become a famous newscaster
- ❏ Be a sex symbol
- ❏ Become a Disney Channel actress
- ❏ Be a famous artist

> ## "I published a bestselling book."
>
> When I was in college, I used to bind collections of my poetry together with a needle and thread and sell them to my friends for a couple of bucks. When I held my first *real* book—from a real publishing house and with national media attention—it still hadn't sunk in. But when someone recognized me on the street, that's when I knew that my book was making me famous. —M. M.

❑ Be on *Survivor*
❑ Be quoted in *The New York Times*
✪ **Become a supermodel**
❑ Achieve a major medical breakthrough
❑ Be chosen as *Time* magazine's Person of the Year
❑ Be inducted into the Country Music Hall of Fame
❑ Sing the national anthem at the World Series
❑ Audition for *Sesame Street*
❑ Discover a new planet
❑ Save the world through science
❑ Create an award-winning television series
❑ Perform with Cirque du Soleil
✪ **Be on Broadway**
❑ Discover a small island

- ❏ Direct a commercial that plays during the Super Bowl
- ❏ Be elected president of the United States of America
- ❏ Walk the red carpet
- ❏ Have some crazy tabloid rumor made up about me
- ❏ Be the next Andy Warhol
- ❏ Win an Emmy
- ❏ Host a talk show

Win a world record

You don't need to be the fastest runner or the tallest man in the world to get yourself in *Guinness World Records*. Amassing extravagant collections, organizing massive gatherings, and cooking giant food makes breaking a world record within reach. Search for fun world records to beat at www.guinnessworldrecords.com and then start e-mailing everyone you know, because whether it's organizing the world's longest conga line (1,048 participants), frying up the largest omelet (6,510 pounds), or adding to the largest collection of traffic cones (137 cones), you're going to need some help.

"I was on *Jeopardy!*"

The audition process was pretty easy—fifty questions at about the $1,600 level of the game. Everyone who got at least thirty-five right got to stay and play a mock game so the contestant coordinators could see a little more of your personality. Then your name goes into a file and if you're lucky, you get picked! I was on the show in 2002 and won twice. —M. Y.

❏ Be a famous underground hip-hop artist
❏ Have a sandwich named after me
○ **Write my own advice column**
❏ Rent a billboard and put my face on it
❏ Have a TV show on public access
❏ Win a gold medal at the Olympics
❏ Write a novel that becomes part of the literary canon
❏ Found my own library
❏ Have a poem written about me
❏ Be a guest on the *Daily Show*
❏ Release a best-selling album
❏ Be in a shampoo commercial
❏ Become anonymously famous

- ❏ Become a Victoria's Secret model
- ❏ Go on the *Jerry Springer* show
- ❏ Sing a duet with William Shatner
- ❏ Be a TV chef and teach people how to cook wonderful things
- ❏ Take a famous photo
- ❏ Be a plus-size model
- ❏ Be culturally significant
- ❏ Gain fame from doing good works
- ❏ Send in my application for a TV reality show
- ❏ Get a leading role in a movie
- ❏ Headline at the Laugh Factory in Hollywood
- ❏ Be followed by paparazzi
- ❏ Win the Nobel Peace Prize
- ❏ Become a famous architect
- ✪ **Be a rock star**
- ❏ Sing a duet with Barbra Streisand
- ❏ Show my collection during New York Fashion Week
- ❏ Become a household name
- ❏ Be a famous rapper
- ❏ Appear in a James Bond film
- ❏ Have a theorem named after me
- ✪ **Win an Oscar**

Name a star named after yourself

There are about 100 billion stars in the Milky Way galaxy alone. Since the earth's population is 6.6 billion, there are more than enough twinkling lights in our galaxy for every man, woman, and child on the planet to have a star named in their honor. Naming a star after yourself, or someone you love, allows you to claim a special spot in the cosmos. You'll get a kit with a certificate of the star name, date, and coordinates, a chart illustrating the star's location, and an astronomy booklet so you can quickly point out your star in the heavens. (Keep in mind that this naming process is largely symbolic—scientists will not be alerted to the fact that a particular star is now named Alex P. Keaton.) Stars can be named through registries such as StarMoniker.com and StarRegistry.com.

❑ Have my own TV show
❑ See my name in lights
❑ Star in a soap opera
❑ Headline a tour
❑ Appear on *The Late Show with David Letterman*
❑ Have a building named after me
✪ **Have a song written about me**

Be an extra

Being a movie or TV extra is a way to begin earning money as an actor, get comfortable being on a set, and potentially launch your acting career. (Brad Pitt, Jackie Chan, and Matt Damon all started as extras.) Here's what you need to do to appear on the big screen, if only for a few seconds.

It helps if you live in or near cities with booming film industries, such as L.A., New York, Toronto, or Vancouver. But if camera crews aren't crawling around your neck of the woods, keep your eye on the trade papers like *Back Stage* magazine's "The Ross Report," which has a pretty comprehensive list of films and TV shows shooting on location (www.backstage.com). Or search casting call listings at TheRightCast.com. If you live near New York or Los Angeles, register with a casting company that specializes in background actors such as CentralCasting.org. Your resume and photo will be kept on file, and you'll be contacted when there's work.

❑ Be on *Saturday Night Live*
☯ **Be a famous singer**
❑ Be on the cover of *Vogue*

- ❏ Be famous for being famous
- ❏ Have my own cooking show
- ❏ Be a celebrity blogger
- ❏ Be dubbed a visionary
- ❏ Win a national Teacher of the Year award
- ❏ Be honored at the White House
- ❏ Be famous for being infamous
- ✪ **Paint a masterpiece**
- ❏ Become a local legend
- ❏ Leave a lasting legacy

36

"Call it a clan, call it a network, call it a tribe, call it a family: Whatever you call it, whoever you are, you need one."

—*Jane Howard, writer*

Have a **Family**

Whether yours resembles the Brady Bunch or the Kennedys, family is a big part of life. As a member of a clan, you have the opportunity to nurture and influence the personal development of others. And if you're lucky, you can take comfort in the notion that whenever you feel lost or lonely, there is a small corner in the great jigsaw puzzle of life where you fit perfectly. Family can also be what you make it: a close-knit group of friends, honorary aunts and uncles, godparents, and adopted children and grandparents. So ponder ways to expand your tribe and grow your family tree diagonally, sideways, and vertically through adoption, foster care, and births. Because having someone to nurture is one of the biggest and best decisions you'll ever make.

- ❑ Teach my son something new every day
- ❑ Be an aunt like Auntie Mame
- ❑ Make damn well sure that my kids are the most important people in my life
- ❑ Take care of my parents when they are older
- ❑ Teach my kids how to express love
- ❑ Become the kind of father that my father was to me
- ❑ Build a tree house for my kids
- ❑ Spend more time alone with my husband
- ❑ Give my kids opportunities that I didn't have
- ❑ Take charge of my fertility
- ❑ Teach my son to ride a bike

✪ **Be a father**

- ❑ Adopt a child who needs me as much as I need him
- ❑ Be a godparent
- ❑ Teach my kids to trust themselves
- ❑ Take a family portrait with my whole extended family
- ❑ Adopt my spouse's kids

✪ **Be a stay-at-home mom**

- ❑ Schedule time to play with my children at least 30 minutes each day

> ## "I've gotten much closer to my grandparents."
>
> I already knew they were great people, but I wanted to know them on a friend level. My grandfather was a great artist, so I asked him about some of his artwork, and that led to a deep conversation about our tastes in art. He is so interesting, I could sit and talk to him for hours. We have a date to go to some museums on my next day off. My grandmother and I have had some good conversations, too. I asked her for some relationship advice, because I figured she must know something since she's been married to my grandfather for fifty years! She's so spunky and funny, and I love taking advice from her.   —A. A.

- ❏ Have a happy, healthy pregnancy
- ❏ Introduce my kids to nature
- ❏ Give my mom everything she needs and wants
- ❏ Help my daughter have better self-esteem
- ❏ Find a great nanny
- ❏ Take a walk with my kids every day
- ❏ Be a grandfather
- ❏ Prepare the nursery
- ❏ Teach my kids to think outside the box

Keep in touch over long distances

Staying in touch with grandchildren and nieces and nephews despite living across the state, country, or world is challenging, but with a little creativity and modern technology you can maintain a close connection. Here are some suggestions:

- For young children, regularly videotape yourself reading books or putting on puppet shows for them.
- Be part of a busy teenager's life by getting comfortable with the technology kids use to keep in touch. Instant messaging, Web cams, photo sharing, and e-mails are the easiest way to reach out, even if it's just to ask "What's up?"
- Send a monthly "thinking of you" care package. Designate a manila envelope for interesting articles, funny jokes, silly comic strips, and other odds and ends you come across over the course of the month that make you think of your relative. When it's nice and fat, stick it in the mail with a little note.
- Start a family scrapbook. Send it to a family member, have them add two pages, and then have them send it on!

✪ **Have twins**

❑ Help my kids be confident

❑ Find a sperm donor

❑ Deliver my baby using the Lamaze method

❑ Go out to dinner with my parents once a week

❑ Take a year off after I have kids and take care
of them

✪ **Have a son**

❑ Come to an agreement with my partner about
having kids

❑ Make sure my kids know I love them

❑ Cook Thanksgiving dinner for my family

❑ Create a clan

❑ Experience the joy of motherhood

❑ Teach my kids to avoid the mistakes I made

❑ Reconcile my differences with my family

❑ Make sure my kids can go to college

❑ Help my son find himself

❑ Make sure my kids know that smart is cool

❑ Be a better mother than my mother was to me

❑ Stop fighting with my sister

✪ **Have a healthy baby**

❑ Teach my kids to appreciate what they have

❑ Be more patient with my daughter

- ❑ Allow my family to teach me new things about myself
- ❑ Breast-feed
- ❑ Take my kids camping
- ❑ Help my daughter grow into a wise and generous person
- ❑ Adopt my nephew
- ❑ Entertain my friend's kids with a puppet show
- ✪ **Have a baby girl**
- ❑ Accept my in-laws as family
- ❑ Tell my friends how much I love them
- ❑ Take a parenting class
- ❑ Teach my son to write his name
- ❑ Help my daughter find her dream job
- ✪ **Have another baby**
- ❑ Teach my son to play guitar

"Having kids is an adventure."

Sharing life with a spouse, raising children, being consumed by love and desire and well wishes for the future of these young ones. Watching them grow, and hoping to guide them in good ways. Absolutely worth it. Absolutely not for the squeamish. Absolutely impossible to prepare for.   —V. N.

Celebrate a holiday with your "chosen family."

Your chosen family is a group of friends, coworkers, or neighbors who support one another, may fight but quickly forgive, and love one another without reserve. Celebrate that connection by finding a holiday to spend together each year, and create some new traditions. Pick holidays like Easter, Halloween, or the Fourth of July, when people are less likely to travel to see their far-away relatives.

❑ See a fertility specialist
❑ Have a water birth
❑ Spend quality time with my daughters
❑ Take the kids folk dancing every week
❑ Teach my kids to make snow angels
❑ Have a big family
❑ Spend every holiday this year with my family
❑ Teach my kids to follow their passions
❑ Have friends that are like family
✪ **Be a mother**
❑ Raise my son to be a good man
❑ Teach my kids about money
❑ Raise my children to be happy and productive adults

☐ Form an urban tribe
☐ Be a surrogate mother
☐ Tell my daughter I love her each and every day

Adopt a grandparent

Add a new member, or several, to your family by adopting a grandparent.

■ Become a pen pal to seniors at EldersWithoutWalls.com, where you can peruse listings of people who would like to be your adopted grandparent.

■ Volunteer at an assisted-living facility, senior center, or nursing home in your community.

■ Contribute to organizations that help the elderly in third world countries such as Adopt-a-Grandparent (www.adopt-a-grandparent.org). Although you don't have direct contact with beneficiaries, your $100 donation pays to take seniors on outings.

■ Check for adopt-a-grandparent programs in your city. If there isn't one, look for a model in Atlanta (www.adoptagrandparent.org), Brooklyn (www.volunteernyc.org), or Seattle (www.elderfriends.org).

> ## "I believe that family is what you make it."
>
> I know when I made "have a family" a goal, I was thinking about the whole husband, kids, and American dream thing. But the longer it stays on my list, the more I think family is really what you make it. So I should just be happy with the relatives and friends I have.　　—S. D.

- ❏ Have another baby
- ❏ Take the kids ice-skating once a week
- ❏ Love the family I have and the family I could possibly have
- ❏ Spend more time with my extended family
- ❏ Be an emergency foster parent
- ❏ Coach my son's Little League team
- ❏ Be a grandmother
- ❏ Get more training as a foster parent
- ❏ Make my family realize that we have everything we need in each other

37

"If you want to understand today,
you have to search yesterday."

—*Pearl Buck*

Document **My Life**

Keeping track of the moments, people, and places that make up your life is a way to bring focus to something that can often feel random and messy. Keeping a journal, whether over several years or just a few months, increases your awareness of daily events, provides an outlet for self-expression, and serves as a record for the future. If you're not into writing, start with simple projects like taking a photo every day for a while or jotting down times when you laughed until you cried. Branch out and adopt goals such as working on a family tree, or seize the moment and do an oral history with your aging relatives. Because knowing where you come from and where you've been makes the journey all the more meaningful.

❏ Capture everyone I love in a single photograph

✪ **Keep a journal**

❏ Make a list of all the books I've read

❏ Write a letter to my future self

❏ Buy a box to store my memories

❏ Take Polaroids of every house I've ever lived in

✪ **Put together an autobiography in scrapbook form**

❏ Document my grandparents' and parents' lives on tape for future generations

---

"I keep a gratitude journal."

I have described my gratitude almost on a daily basis, and it's a wonderful thing to do. I began to see that there are so many positive, beautiful, good things (and people) in my life. I used to constantly revisit all the bad things that had happened to me, so I was resentful, angry, hurt, and filled with all kinds of negative feelings. Now I've started to see all the good things in my life because of my focus on the positive. I can't even count the benefits I have gained from writing in my gratitude journal.   —F. L.

Tell your own story

If you're one of those people who thinks that nothing interesting has ever happened to you, think again. There is great beauty, humor, and drama to be found in the smallest, most mundane moments. So shine the light on some old memories and recast them into something worth telling.

- Have any scars? What happened?
- Describe your first kiss.
- Describe your first friend. What did you do together?
- When have you been most scared?
- Ever been in trouble? What did you do?
- What was your happiest/saddest moment?
- Describe the rooms in the house you grew up in.

❑ Bury a time capsule
❑ Make a list of 10 songs that were important to me at different times
❑ Take a photo-portrait of every person who visits my apartment
❑ Write a 6-word memoir
❑ Post pictures of the world as seen from my bicycle seat
❑ Document ridiculous dates and pickup lines

- ❑ Transfer family oral history tapes to CD
- ❑ Document kindness, life's selfless acts, beautiful moments, and gentle amusements, and encourage others to do the same
- ❑ Keep an ongoing list of things that make me happy
- ✪ **Publish my autobiography**
- ❑ Take pictures of places that were important to my childhood and put them in an album
- ❑ Scan all my family photos
- ❑ Keep an illustrated journal
- ✪ **Document my baby's first year**
- ❑ Write down my memories of my mom
- ❑ Collect my childhood drawings
- ❑ Maintain a list of all the people I've met around the world and keep in touch
- ❑ Videotape myself doing something crazy
- ❑ Have professional family portraits taken

"I take a photo every day."

It's nearly mid-March, and I have not missed a day!
This lovely little project is really opening my eyes and
making me think! I love it!   —D. A.

Document your travels

Remember places, people, and particular experiences with these suggestions:

- City, state, or highway maps, with routes or places visited marked in red, make great mementos and can be framed and hung on the wall.
- Shot glasses, matchbooks, even holiday ornaments are ways to commemorate a trip.
- Get at least one postcard from each town you visit.
- Document your journey by using online travel journals such as OffExploring.com, MyTripJournal.com, and TravellersPoint.com.

❏ Make a keepsake box for my daughter
❏ Summarize each day in one poetic sentence
❏ Capture my life in the style of a B movie
❏ Chronicle my crazy/interesting dating escapades
❏ Photograph my travels
❏ Write a memoir of my childhood
❏ Keep all of my love letters
✪ **Make a collage of happy memories**
❏ Publish a book of my grandfather's World War II photos

- ❑ Photograph my cooking
- ❑ Keep a list of each day's "highs"
- ❑ Take a picture in front of every state sign
- ❑ Keep a photographic record of the plants, animals, and fungi in my garden
- ❑ Own a world map and mark the places I've visited
- ⊙ **Write down my earliest memories from childhood**
- ❑ Start a website about my travels
- ❑ Edit all my family videos
- ⊙ **Write down a memory a day**
- ❑ Chronicle my commute
- ❑ Write the story of our first year of marriage and read it on our 50th anniversary
- ❑ Write about my Peace Corps experiences
- ❑ Keep a list of nice things people have said to me or about me
- ❑ List all the restaurants I go to
- ❑ Keep a notebook to jot down my ideas
- ❑ Film myself sleeping
- ❑ Create a playlist of my life (so far)
- ❑ List 100 priceless moments in my life
- ❑ List every gift I remember receiving

"I recorded an oral history of my grandmother."

About twenty-five years ago, my dad recorded his parents reminiscing by hiding a tape recorder under the kitchen table. Now that both of them are dead, the tape is important to everyone in the family. About two years ago, I went to my maternal grandmother's house and recorded an interview with her about her early life. No one else knows I did this. She doesn't want them to "until later." I plan to transcribe it soon. If you can get someone to sit down for an hour or two, or if you have to do it without the person knowing, it is definitely worthwhile.   —S. Y.

❑ Keep a daily journal of my relationship with my daughter

❑ Keep a list of my favorite movies

✪ **Blog my memories**

❑ Write my mother's biography

❑ Keep a wine journal

❑ Videotape seemingly boring parts of my day

❑ Create a family keepsake

❑ Write a letter to my kids about what I wish for them and put it away until they're 18

38

"Sex is one of the nine reasons for reincarnation. The other eight are unimportant." —*Henry Miller*

Get It On

It's been a while since society spoke of sexual fantasies and fetishes only behind closed doors. These days, a fun and fanciful sex life, assuming it's done safely and with consenting adults, is something to pursue and enjoy. So if you're harboring lustful thoughts about joining the Mile High Club, betting it all in a game of strip poker, or straying from your usual routine between the sheets, go for it. And for you adventurous types who think you've done it all, there's *always* something new to learn. Find out what gets you hot and bothered, discover what turns your partner on, and bring a little va-va-voom to the bedroom. The sizzle and spark of an erotic thrill is one of life's greatest pleasures. You owe it to yourself to get it on!

- ❑ Try everything once
- ❑ Make out in the middle of a high school football field with the stadium lights still on
- ❑ Have tantric sex
- ❑ Make love on a rooftop
- ❑ Explore bisexuality
- ❑ Have a clearer relationship with my friend with benefits
- ✪ **Have a threesome**
- ❑ Learn to trust my partner's touch
- ❑ Tell my partner my fantasies without being embarrassed
- ❑ Invent a new sex position
- ✪ **Have sex 8 times in 1 day**
- ❑ Have sex in as many random locations as possible
- ❑ Get laid by a supermodel
- ❑ Talk dirty in French

"I joined the Mile High Club."

Not sure this requires any detail, but here's a tip: It's best in the first-class bathroom. The flight attendants don't bother you!　　　　　　　　　　　　　　　—M. M.

Learn to striptease

A striptease is not only a steamy show for your lucky partner, but a great way to embrace your body's sensual side. And even though you're the one baring it all, you're also the one calling the shots, which can be pretty liberating. If you're feeling a little shy, consider taking pole-dancing lessons offered at studios such as S Factor (www.sfactor.com) and many local gyms. A popular new form of exercise, exotic (and erotic) dance moves such as the flagpole, fireman, and flamingo build strength and self-confidence while releasing inhibitions.

❑ Buy more sexy lingerie
❑ Make love on the golf course
❑ Have an affair with a younger man
✪ **French kiss**
❑ Play strip hide-and-seek
❑ Do it in a parking lot at night on the top of a car
❑ Be uninhibited enough to make noise during sex
❑ Make love on a beach
❑ Stop being such a prude
❑ Get it on in the back of a movie theater
❑ Film myself having sex

"I love making love in the woods."

I've done this in several forests, actually. There is something inherently spiritual about having sex in the presence of those old, old trees. Here are a few tips: Take a blanket or two if it's chilly, be prepared to hike a bit to find some real privacy, wear clothing that's easy to get out of—and back into—and bring alcohol-free wet wipes.—G. A.

- ❏ Experiment with multiple partners
- ❏ Do it until the bed breaks
- ❏ Get laid by the end of high school
- ✪ **Make love in the rain**
- ❏ Watch porn together
- ❏ Have an Italian affair
- ❏ Masturbate in front of my partner
- ❏ Make love under the aurora borealis
- ❏ Get laid in Las Vegas
- ❏ Be more playful and inventive in bed
- ❏ Make love in a field of wildflowers
- ❏ Be a sex god
- ❏ Go dirty dancing
- ❏ Make love

❏ Have an orgasm with someone besides my hand
❏ Convert a hetero
❏ Enjoy oral sex
❏ Make out with Pop Rocks
❏ Role-play in the bedroom
❏ Enjoy extended foreplay
❏ Talk dirty in bed
❏ Make love to my professor
❏ Use chocolate sauce in naughty ways
❏ Make whoopee on every continent
✪ **Have orgasms with my partner again**
❏ Get bondage gear
❏ Have a mind-blowingly perfect kiss
❏ Make love in an elevator
❏ Get my groove back
❏ Make slow love

Play strip Twister

Transform Twister from a middle school classic to an adult aphrodisiac by giving the rules an R-rated update and requiring players to remove an article of clothing each time they take a tumble. The words "right hand, blue dot" will take on a whole new meaning.

- ❏ Buy furry handcuffs
- ❏ Learn to come after my girlfriend
- ✪ **Have better orgasms**
- ❏ Make love outdoors
- ❏ Lick whipped cream off my lover
- ❏ Sneak into an ancient monolithic monument and make love
- ✪ **Have a one-night stand**

Try everything in the *Kama Sutra*

An ancient Indian text on love and relationships, the *Kama Sutra* is widely known for the chapter titled "On Sexual Union," which includes descriptions of 250 sexual positions. But the book was written as a how-to guide on marriage, and it includes thirty-five additional chapters covering topics such as physical attraction, pleasure, and spirituality. By combining the spiritual, emotional, and physical aspects of sex into an encyclopedia of love, the *Kama Sutra* not only provides instructions on new positions, but rekindles the romance. The original text, which included only descriptions (no illustrations), can be found at www.freekamasutra.com, but you may find it more fun to thumb through a book with accompanying diagrams.

"I cheated."

Not worth it! This is one of my biggest regrets in life.
Don't do it. If you want to be with someone else, break up
with the person you're with first. At least have the decency
to do that. I didn't and the guilt eats at me every day.—R. N.

❑ Spice up my sex life
❑ Talk to my lover about what I like
❑ Learn how to perform oral sex
❑ Find my G-spot
❑ Surprise my partner at work for a quickie
❑ Have sex in my front yard and not care if the
neighbors see
❑ Have sex with my boss on my desk
❑ Read erotic stories aloud together
❑ Have a passionate love affair

39

"Carefully put two bricks together.
There it begins."

—*Ludwig Mies van der Rohe, architect*

Build Something

Whether it's a cabin constructed with logs you chopped yourself or a Popsicle-stick picture frame, building something proves that your two hands are good for more than typing and channel surfing. Join the D-I-Y nation in turning raw materials into functional (even beautiful) pieces. You don't need to know the difference between a box-end and an open-end wrench to be a builder. There are plenty of simple projects—a rack for spare keys, a planter box for the patio—that can be made with minimal tools. Devote some free time, energy (and depending on how big your project, some blood, sweat, and tears) to building something. Because there's nothing more rewarding than having someone marvel at your driftwood coffee table and being able to say, "I built that myself."

- ❑ Build a letterpress
- ❑ Build a swing set
- ❑ Build something with my kids
- ❑ Build an observatory
- ❑ Build a tepee
- ❑ Build a bar
- ❑ Build a snowman
- ❑ Build something out of wood
- ❑ Build a home theater
- ❑ Build a birdhouse
- ❑ Build a sailboat in a bottle
- ✪ **Build a workshop**
- ❑ Build a maze
- ❑ Build a chicken coop
- ❑ Build a fairy castle out of sugar cubes
- ❑ Design a milk carton boat
- ❑ Build a pergola
- ❑ Build a darkroom
- ❑ Build a dollhouse
- ❑ Build a patio
- ❑ Build an arch-top guitar
- ❑ Build a telescope
- ✪ **Build a catapult**
- ❑ Build a surfboard

"I built my house."

If I had known the full extent of my dream project, I may never have begun. Now, seven months after completion, I look back and see the process as it unfolded and am so happy that I couldn't see the future and let it scare me out of accomplishing my dream!

I completely support anyone who wants to achieve this goal. It is VERY worthwhile and when you're through, you'll walk through the doors of your new home and you'll know every part of the journey from the inside out! Go for it!

—S. S.

❏ Build a submarine
❏ Build something with toothpicks
✪ **Build a secret garden**
❏ Build a wigwam
❏ Build a secret underground lair
❏ Build a pyramid
❏ Build a farmhouse
❏ Build a cello
❏ Build a bathroom
✪ **Build my own eco-house**
❏ Build a marionette

Build a kite

It's a common misperception that strong, stiff winds are the best for kite flying. Many kites are designed for light, breezy weather. The success of your kite depends on the design. Simple kites are little more than a diamond-shaped piece of paper with two sticks forming a cross glued in the center and a piece of string attached to the center of the cross. Find out what designs fly best in certain types of weather, download free kite designs and instructions, and purchase kite kits from the Seattle-based Drachen Foundation at www.drachen.org.

- ❏ Build a chapel
- ❏ Build a road
- ❏ Build a holodeck
- ❏ Build a hotel
- ✪ **Build a supercomputer**
- ❏ Build a dresser
- ❏ Build a motorbike
- ❏ Build a lighthouse
- ❏ Build a school
- ❏ Build a bridge
- ❏ Build a distillery

✪ **Build a sauna**
❏ Build a Harley
❏ Build a mosque
❏ Build a space elevator
✪ **Build a recording studio**
❏ Build a house with secret passageways
❏ Build an aviary
❏ Build an igloo
❏ Build a boomerang
❏ Build a Porsche
❏ Build a bunker
❏ Build an arcade game
❏ Build a library
❏ Build a yacht

"I build furniture."

I have made several pieces of furniture. I'm always amazed at how cheap and crappy store-bought furniture is. I like my furniture to be solid and feel like it will last as long as me. I made my bed. I used ironwood for the posts, which is a very hard timber and makes the bed very solid. There is something very satisfying about working with timber and the smell of freshly cut wood. —J. N.

Build a terrarium

Brighten your home with a small indoor garden.
Terrariums are collections of plants cultivated in clear
containers such as large jars, aquariums, or vases.
To assemble a terrarium, follow these steps:

1. Cover ½ inch to 1½ inches of the container bottom
   with gravel.
2. Cover the gravel with a piece of window screen,
   nylon hosiery, or other synthetic fabric.
3. Fill approximately one fifth of the container with
   potting soil.
4. Arrange plants inside the container. (Check out
   CanadianGardening.com for a list of plants that
   thrive in terrariums.) Consider height, texture,
   and color when making your selections. If you
   want to view the plants from all sides, place the
   tallest plants in the center. For containers with
   one side against a wall, place the tallest plants
   in the back.
5. Arrange decorative stones around the plants.
6. Water the plants sparingly, close the container,
   and put the terrarium in indirect sunlight.

❏ Build a monument

❏ Build my own Trojan horse

❏ Build an entire town out of gingerbread

❏ Build my own sanctuary

✪ **Build an airplane**

❏ Build a home theater

❏ Build some of my crazy inventions

❏ Build a geodesic greenhouse

❏ Build a better search engine

❏ Build a rock-climbing wall

❏ Build a prefab house in the desert

❏ Build a go-cart

❏ Build a giant hedge maze in my front yard

❏ Build a flying car

❏ Build miniatures

❏ Build a church

❏ Build a toolshed

✪ **Build a school in Africa**

❏ Build a hovercraft

❏ Build a gyrocopter

✪ **Build a secret tree house**

❏ Build a sailboat

❏ Build a sweat lodge

❏ Build an art car

- ❑ Build a Web application
- ❑ Build an ark
- ❑ Build a model sailboat from scratch and sail it in Central Park
- ❑ Build a rose garden
- ✪ **Build clocks**
- ❑ Build a windmill
- ❑ Build my own oscilloscope
- ❑ Build a pagoda
- ✪ **Build a website**
- ❑ Build a radio
- ❑ Build an aquarium
- ❑ Build an end table
- ❑ Build a workbench
- ❑ Build a sand castle
- ❑ Build a rocking chair
- ❑ Build a fort
- ✪ **Build a canoe**
- ❑ Build a clubhouse
- ❑ Build a Japanese garden with a stone bridge
- ❑ Build a porch
- ❑ Build a fire pit
- ❑ Build a toy box for my grandkids
- ❑ Build a planter for the deck

Build something with your kids

Craft and construction projects are great for keeping busy bodies entertained and teaching little ones new skills. BuildEazy.com has free online instructions for children's building projects, including a kid-size picnic table and scooter. Books such as Eric Stromer's *Do-It-Yourself Family* give instructions on how to renovate every room in the house with the help of kids and spouses. *The Kids' Building Workshop: 15 Woodworking Projects for Kids and Parents to Build Together*, by Craig Robertson, is perfect for children in grades 3–7 and provides how-to information on building a birdcage, toolbox, stool, and other projects.

❏ Build a loom
❏ Build a foosball table
✪ **Build a time machine**
❏ Build a solar-powered car
❏ Build a theme park
❏ Build a smoker
❏ Build a fort out of Lincoln Logs

40

"Education is the most powerful weapon which you can use to change the world." —*Nelson Mandela*

Continue
My Education

Not to sound too much like your seventh-grade science teacher, but your brain is a muscle—it needs exercise to stay in shape. Don't let that beautiful mind of yours go to waste. Keep on learning to give your brain a much-needed workout—not only will you become a more flexible and discerning thinker, but it just might change your life. Jump from underling to the corner office by completing an advanced-degree program. Return to campus and get that philosophy degree you've always wanted. Or sign up for a course and discover a passion or an ability you never knew you had. The value of education is immeasurable. It's one of those rare experiences that is both a means to an end and an end in itself. It's up to you to take advantage of that killer combination—your brain will thank you.

- ☐ Take a grant-writing workshop
- ☐ Double major
- ☐ Homeschool my kids
- ☐ Get a Ph.D.
- ✪ **Go to college**
- ☐ Study homeopathic medicine
- ☐ Earn an online degree
- ☐ Take the GMAT and apply to business school
- ☐ Stay on the dean's list until I graduate
- ☐ Go to school in Japan
- ☐ Study miming
- ☐ Enroll in a real estate course
- ☐ Get a degree in architecture
- ☐ Finish my college applications
- ☐ Major in zoology
- ☐ Get accepted into dental school
- ☐ Go to cooking school in France
- ☐ Get a master's degree in library science
- ☐ Study botany
- ☐ Learn to be an expert bartender
- ✪ **Take an art class**
- ☐ Study every day
- ☐ Attend a poetry workshop
- ☐ Study cinematography

"I graduated college."

Yesterday I walked at my graduation ceremony. It brought tears of joy to my eyes, first in the processional as the band played "Pomp and Circumstance," and again when people threw their caps into the air. It felt incredible when we switched the tassel from the right side of the cap to the left. Two years ago I set the goal of doing this in two years, and I've done it. I will carry the warmth of this day with me for a long time.　　　　　　　　　　　—R. T.

❏ Do well on the GRE
❏ Take a course in race-car driving
❏ Study textiles
❏ Educate myself in economic policy
❏ Go to massage therapy school
❏ Study astronomy
✪ **Take piano lessons**
❏ Study at an ashram
❏ Increase my computer proficiency
❏ Go to beauty school
❏ Apply for financial aid
❏ Learn how to make a dress
✪ **Study Buddhism**

"I went back to school as an older student."

I decided to go back to college to study acting. I've wanted to act since I was ten years old. When I walked into the first class, I thought, "This must be the wrong class—it's full of kids!" It made me feel really self-conscious, but gradually, I made friends and, contrary to my fears, my age was no issue at all! Going to college has really boosted my confidence and given me the courage to take a huge step toward achieving my goal. We just had four sell-out performances of our latest show. The sky is the limit!

—K. E.

❑ Become an Egyptologist
❑ Major in linguistics
❑ Graduate summa cum laude
✪ **Get my GED**
❑ Study history
❑ Take a course in creative writing
❑ Major in music
❑ Earn my degree in accounting
❑ Change my major
❑ Go to clown college

❑ Go to West Point
❑ Discover the art of wine tasting
❑ Take a jewelry-making course
❑ Get into medical school
❑ Write my dissertation
❑ Take an online course for college credit
❑ Get my master's degree before I'm 30
❑ Create my own college major
❑ Study fashion
✪ **Make the dean's list**
❑ Get accepted into an art school
❑ Major in neuroscience
❑ Get a degree in my 50s
❑ Take a course in interior design
❑ Major in fine arts
❑ Study at Oxford
❑ Get accepted into a school of my choice
❑ Major in Japanese
✪ **Write my thesis**
❑ Receive my engineering degree
❑ Take a public-speaking course
❑ Major in psychology
❑ Take at least one continuing education course
  per year

- ❑ Study acupuncture
- ✪ **Get a second degree**
- ❑ Study meteorology
- ❑ Immerse myself in Spanish culture
- ✪ **Take advantage of my employer's continuing education program**
- ❑ Study animation
- ❑ Go to a private school
- ❑ Take a music-appreciation course
- ❑ Get a degree in marine biology
- ❑ Study criminology
- ❑ Earn a degree in social work
- ❑ Take a leatherworking course
- ❑ Study and practice yoga at an ashram

"I learned a new language."

I had always wanted to learn a foreign language to the point of fluency, but it's really tough to do unless you totally immerse yourself in it. I didn't have that opportunity until well into my adult life, and then it was also a matter of necessity, as I had moved to Sweden. Take it from me: Old dogs CAN learn new tricks—they just have to work a bit harder at it!   —S. Z.

Develop better study habits

Choose the most effective study habits for your learning style. The basic learning styles are auditory, receiving information by listening; visual, reading about a subject; and kinesthetic, learning through hands-on activities. Think about how you learn best and then improve your study habits with these tips.

- Auditory pupils will find recording and replaying lectures or repeating information with their eyes closed helpful.
- Visual learners benefit from color-coding notes and writing outlines.
- Kinesthetic students should join study groups, use flash cards, and develop memory techniques that require movement.

✪ Go to nursing school
❑ Study politics
❑ Be a film major
❑ Take a management course
❑ Learn how to rock climb
✪ Study anthropology
❑ Get accepted to a school in Ireland

- ❑ Go to flight school
- ❑ Study nutrition
- ❑ Get my master's degree
- ❑ Take a beginner hang-gliding course
- ❑ Become a semiotician
- ❑ Study genetics
- ❑ Learn to fence
- ❑ Study accounting
- ✪ **Get a law degree**
- ❑ Learn flower arrangement
- ❑ Become an expert in etiquette

Go to cooking school

Restaurant and catering careers aren't the only tasty reasons to attend cooking school. Those skilled in the culinary arts possess the know-how to get picky kids to actually enjoy broccoli and spinach, bring joy to holidays with sumptuous feasts, and make every meal special. If you want to expand your vegan repertoire or finally master a perfect soufflé, take a class at a local restaurant or kitchen-supply store. If your dream is to open a five-star restaurant, check out AllCulinarySchools.com to find courses that fit your budget and needs.

❑ Study theology

❑ Major in journalism

❑ Get my teaching certificate in special education

❑ Study in Paris

✪ **Get a degree in computer science**

❑ Take a stained-glass making course

❑ Learn Web design

❑ Take a course with Elderhostel

❑ Attend the New York Film Academy

❑ Take a marketing course

❑ Earn a degree in graphic design

❑ Stay in school

41

"Be brave. Take risks. Nothing can substitute for experience." —*Paulo Coelho*

Do Something Daring

Protected and dulled by daily routines, deep-rooted habits, and a tried-and-true way of living, the walls of your comfort zone grow a little thicker with each passing day. But why settle for the same-old, same-old when there's so much fun to be had? There are pranks to pull, parties to crash, inhibitions to shed, phobias to confront, and chances to take! So what if it makes you feel awkward, shakes up the status quo, or causes a little trouble? And so what if people stare or scold or are shocked out of their conventional skins? Risk taking is like doing push-ups for the soul—it makes you strong. So be bold. Be brave. We double-dog dare you!

- ❏ Gamble nonstop for 48 hours in Las Vegas
- ✪ **Crash a party**
- ❏ Do something that surprises, inspires, and terrifies me
- ❏ Take a double-dog dare
- ❏ Eat alone in public
- ❏ Scream my secrets from a rooftop
- ❏ Find the courage to tell my dad I'm not a Republican
- ❏ Smoke apple tobacco from a hookah
- ❏ Drink absinthe
- ❏ Ask for a raise
- ❏ Throw a pie in someone's face
- ❏ Crowd-surf
- ❏ Ride a mechanical bull
- ❏ Eat alligator meat
- ✪ **Go streaking**
- ❏ Try paintball
- ❏ Perform karaoke
- ❏ Take a ride in a vintage biplane
- ❏ Ask someone out on a date
- ❏ Try peyote
- ❏ Cast a magical spell
- ❏ Discuss sex very loudly in a restaurant

"I go skinny-dipping at night"

I live in a seaside town where there are little rock pools along the coast. Some nights in summer I go for a walk with no intention to swim, but the water is so beautiful, I decide to strip and have a swim. The other evening just as the sun set, I bobbed up and down and watched the pink streaky sky change to orange and fade to dark blue and black. I dried off in the air and put my clothes on before walking home feeling beautiful and refreshed.   —P. T.

- ❑ Make a half-court shot backwards
- ❑ Hold hands in public
- ❑ Have a séance in a cemetery
- ❑ Street perform
- ✪ **Do a striptease**
- ❑ Repair my tiara and wear it in public
- ❑ Sneak into a movie theater
- ❑ Wear a beehive hairdo in public
- ❑ Never follow the crowd
- ❑ Stand up for those who can't stand up for themselves
- ✪ **Get a divorce**
- ❑ Sneak backstage at a concert
- ❑ Wear a crazy hat in public

"I danced in a public fountain."

I was seventeen, a little timid, traveling abroad for the first time. It was 1994 and Sweden was playing in the World Cup. I went with some friends into Stockholm to watch the game in a bar. When the game ended and Sweden was victorious, thousands of people simultaneously flooded out of the bars and into the streets singing "We Are the Champions." Strangers were kissing, everyone was dancing. It was a warm summer night, so lots of people jumped into the fountains of downtown Stockholm, and I jumped in along with them and danced in the water with a random handsome stranger. Just then a bright light went off. The next day, there I was on the front page of the *Aftonbladet* newspaper.　　　　　　　　　　　　　—O. V.

❑ Sneak into a club
❑ Find the courage to go home
✪ **Go on a blind date**
❑ Bet $100 on black on a roulette wheel in Vegas
❑ Steal someone's lawn gnome
❑ Hit all the buttons in a crowded elevator
❑ Own a pair of leather chaps
❑ Show more skin

❏ Wear bright red lipstick with bright red nails

❏ Perform in a musical

✪ **Sneak out**

❏ Drag race for pink slips

❏ Spray paint a billboard

❏ Have the courage to approach my crush

❏ Pose nude

❏ Go to networking events alone

❏ Egg a passing car

❏ Love without fear

✪ **Join a protest**

❏ Be courageous even if it means being unpopular

❏ Dress in drag

❏ Spray champagne on someone

❏ Sneak into a trial and shout "Objection!"

❏ Try anything once

❏ Fight a cage match

❏ Run through the sprinklers when I'm 80

❏ Sabotage somebody's car with a banana

❏ Make prank calls

✪ **Pick a lock**

❏ Sneak a porcupine into a petting zoo

❏ Steal kisses

❏ Tag a public wall

- ☐ Cause mayhem
- ☐ Toilet paper a house
- ☐ Get into a fistfight
- ☐ Play golf through a hotel lobby
- ☐ Buy a stranger a drink in a bar
- ☐ Have a bark-off with someone's annoying dog
- ✪ **Sing "I Will Always Love You" to someone I've never met**
- ☐ Organize a heist
- ☐ Fork someone's yard

Eat blowfish

Coveted for its distinctive taste and notorious for its lethal flesh, blowfish is the ultimate act of epicurean derring-do. The big-eyed species contains a potent neurotoxin that causes asphyxiation and has no known antidote. In North America, the blowfish served in restaurants undergoes a multilayered inspection process and is considered to be no more harmful than sushi. If you're brave enough to play dining roulette, visit Japan, where the only safety regulation is requiring highly trained chefs to prepare the life-threatening delicacy. Choose the restaurant and chef carefully or blowfish could be your last meal.

"I went on a road trip with no destination."

Right after I graduated college, with no serious plans, I decided to just drive west until I found a good place to stop. I picked up a friend of a friend at the last minute, complete with dog, and off we drove in my little Nissan. Wouldn't trade that experience for anything. Lots of craziness, lots of good times, fantastic experience. In my journeys, I've seen the Corn Palace, a dinosaur park, caravans, Graceland (Elvis lives!), national parks, and, well, just a ton of cool stuff. Definitely more fun in groups, but enjoyable alone (though not for the faint of heart).   —N. F.

❏ Throw snowballs at couples as they walk by
❏ Have a tabloid fight with someone famous
❏ Crash a wedding
❏ Kidnap someone on their birthday
✪ **Have the courage to apologize**
❏ Trespass on abandoned property
❏ Ride naked on horseback
❏ Sing loudly and terribly out of tune
❏ Make a stupid noise in public, then hide and
    blame someone else

Go on a blind date

Talking to strangers requires confidence. Going on a blind date takes courage. Sure, the odds are stacked against you, but as any gambler will tell you, that's just when things start to get interesting. Keep your expectations low (you don't have to fall in love on the first date), plan ahead to eliminate awkward moments, keep the conversation light, and focus on the fun. Most important, don't take it all so seriously. You're playing dating roulette, so date in volume—there's always the chance that you'll win big.

- ❏ Swim in the deep end
- ❏ Go on a spontaneous road trip
- ❏ Do a dance routine with my friends in a public place
- ✪ **Get over my stage fright**
- ❏ Participate in an act of civil disobedience
- ❏ Go to a nude beach
- ❏ Have a lingerie party
- ❏ Run a kissing booth
- ❏ Tell my boss that he is wrong
- ❏ Climb more . . . and don't be so scared of falling

Do Something **Daring**

❏ Sleep on the street for a night
❏ Gamble more than I can afford to lose
❏ Let my hair go gray
❏ Spill my guts to a complete stranger
❏ Practice witchcraft
❏ Wear a beret in public
✪ **Leave the rat race**
❏ Take the road less traveled
❏ Skip a class
❏ Move away from my hometown
❏ Admit when I'm wrong
❏ Say yes more often
❏ Confront my roommate
❏ Move to a city where I don't know anyone
❏ Go back to school
❏ Tell a stranger a joke
❏ Find the courage to leave my job
❏ Write my name in wet cement
❏ Ask myself each morning, "How will I be brave today?"

42

"Genius begins great works;
labor alone finishes them."

—Joseph Joubert, philosopher

Finish What I Start

Academic degrees a few credits short of completion, half-done home improvements, a dozen nearly finished craft projects. Chances are you have a couple of things growing dusty on your permanent to-do list. Before you launch a take-no-prisoners mission to finally restore an old desk or finish that dissertation, take a moment to review your goals (both big and small) with a critical eye. Every six months or so, be a ferocious editor and cross off the things that aren't worth worrying about anymore and underline the things that have remained unfinished for far too long. Move them to the top of your list and jot down at least three additional steps you need to take to get you closer to completion. The "right time" might never come, so why not do it now?

- ❑ Finish paying off my college loans
- ❑ Finish recording my album
- ✪ **Finish my portfolio**
- ❑ Finish a marathon
- ❑ Finish getting my pilot's license
- ❑ Finish getting my GED
- ❑ Finish painting my house
- ❑ Finish my business plan and stick to it
- ✪ **Finish writing my book—and get it published**
- ❑ Finish building the backyard deck
- ❑ Finish my poems
- ❑ Finish a painting
- ❑ Finish an entire day's to-do list
- ❑ Finish fencing our yard
- ✪ **Finish preparing the house for the baby**
- ❑ Finish my robot
- ❑ Finish at least one of my songs
- ❑ Finish remodeling the bathroom
- ❑ Finish my symphony
- ❑ Finish a crossword puzzle
- ❑ Finish unpacking . . . so I can start decorating!
- ❑ Finish knitting my scarf

"I finished a sewing project."

It was curious picking up the needle and thread again and trying to make nice, even stitches, and then after a while it started feeling natural. And then I got really excited because I realized that I started sewing because of a friend, but I continued sewing because I really, really liked it— and it just came back to me like the old "riding a bicycle" thing. In one afternoon, I finished the final seams of a project (a pair of Victorian drawers—very cute with lace and pink ribbon) and ta-daa! I am one step closer to finishing *all* my sewing projects!   —M. D.

❏ Finish reading the Bible
✪ **Finish decorating my house**
❏ Finish reading Proust
❏ Finish my Invisalign and have straight teeth
❏ Finish adolescence
❏ Finish my sentences
❏ Finish my wedding thank-you notes
❏ Finish my 1,000-piece jigsaw puzzle
❏ Finish writing my memoir
❏ Finish law school and don't feel weird about not becoming an attorney

Get the job done

Finishing up craft and home repair projects is one of the most common goals on 43 Things members' lists. And it's easy to see why. Bungee jumping out of a helicopter is a goal to get excited about—but finish tiling the bathroom? Not so fun. Here are some ways to finish the job:

1. Keep progress moving on a bathroom or kitchen remodel by scheduling a dinner party. A social event gives you something to look forward to and keeps you on track.

2. Come up with some consequences for not finishing, such as sacrificing small pleasures like a movie with friends if you miss the deadline. Or enforce a friendly punishment like buying a round of drinks at happy hour.

3. Schedule a block of time each week to work on your project. Break the task into smaller goals—knit six rows a day, clean out one corner of the garage, organize a single box of photos.

❑ Finish my sculpture
❑ Finish rehab
❑ Finish reading the newspaper every day
❑ Finish my divorce
❑ Finish my quilt

- ❏ Finish building my coffin
- ❏ Finish restoring all the furniture I've been collecting
- ❏ Finish paying off my car
- ❏ Finish filing all my paperwork
- ❏ Finish my spring cleaning
- ❏ Finish applying for disability
- ❏ Finish my doula certification coursework
- ❏ Finish typing my grandfather's memories
- ❏ Finish building my house
- ✪ **Finish my model railroad**

"I finished my dissertation."

Albert Ellis's book *Overcoming Procrastination* was the catalyst for a real revelation that led me to finish the dissertation: the idea that I could fail. Here's the idea: So, you fail to finish. What is the absolute worst consequence? For me it was the shame of telling my friends and family. I pictured the humiliating scenes of confession, the condescension, and the disappointment. But then I realized that most of them had assumed for years now that I wouldn't finish anyway. And somehow I found great freedom in this thought—the idea that I could fail; in fact, that in some ways I already had failed and had survived it. —S. H.

- [ ] Finish paying back my parents
- [ ] Finish my baby quilt *before* the baby is born
- [ ] Finish a game of Monopoly
- [ ] Finish my 5-week boot camp workout—and do it again!
- [ ] Finish weeding the vegetable garden
- [ ] Finish dive master class
- [ ] Finish building the goat barn
- [ ] Finish my Renaissance fair costume
- [ ] Finish the half-done jobs around the house
- [ ] Finish all the books I didn't finish in school
- [ ] Finish getting my broker's license
- [ ] Finish writing my play
- ⊙ **Finish my thesis**

"I'm ready to finish mourning."

I'm ready to start moving forward. My grief will be with me for the rest of my life, but I'm not thrown by it like I was before. I have a measure of control now. I know what the pitfalls are, such as feeling sorry for myself and mindlessly pursuing the past. I am accepting of how things are, I'm open to how things will be, and I'm starting to leave my life with my wife behind.   —P. Y.

Stop procrastinating

Procrastination keeps you from getting the job done and
makes you feel anxious and guilty. So why are we all so good
at it? Unlearn your procrastination skills with these tips:

- Focus on the starting line instead of the finish line.
  Define the first step. Projects are often composed of a
  series of smaller tasks, so identify the first and next
  steps and get satisfaction from checking them off.
- Allow for do-overs, and view larger projects as a series
  of beginnings. If you get distracted while working on a
  task, don't scold yourself. Just start again.
- Meticulous overplanning can become a form of
  procrastination—it feels like you're working, but really
  you haven't begun.
- Schedule in leisure time. Promise yourself that you will
  take a break after fifteen minutes. Or plan a day at the
  beach on Sunday after a full day's work on Saturday.

❑ Finish putting my favorite recipes on recipe cards
❑ Finish my teaching certification coursework
❑ Finish my family tree
❑ Finish restoring my sailboat

43

"It's only with the heart that one can see rightly; what is most important is invisible to the eye."

—*Antoine de Saint Exupéry*

100 Things that
Make Me Happy
(Besides Money)

All the recent happiness studies have proved that people with lots of money are no happier than the rest of us. Money can buy lots of things that make life easier or more interesting or more fun—but it can't buy happiness. In an effort to remember this fact, thousands of 43 Things members made it a goal to "Identify 100 Things that Make Me Happy (Besides Money)." One hundred small, everyday pleasures—those satisfying things that make you grin, make you feel cozy, make you feel that "all is well with the world." Similar to writing down goals, listing life's gratuitous perks clarifies what's important and makes you appreciate these moments. When your mood starts to darken, read over your own list, add to it, and remind yourself of all the simple little things that make you smile.

- [ ] The way pages of really old books smell
- [ ] Getting packages in the mail
- [ ] A girls' night *in*
- [ ] The sound of waves crashing
- [ ] How cute my toenails look right after I paint them, before I ruin them five minutes later
- [ ] Hearing juicy gossip
- [ ] Skateboarding
- [ ] Walking through an empty park on a chilly spring day
- [ ] Ice cream in the summer
- [ ] Exercising with a friend
- [ ] Being selfless
- [ ] My bedroom when it's clean
- [ ] Roller coasters
- [ ] Dancing all night with friends
- [ ] Not having to go to school
- [ ] Seeing my little brother smile
- [ ] Lilac bushes
- [ ] The smell of my apartment when I first walk in
- [ ] Dive-bombing into a pool or lake
- [ ] Swings and slides at a playground
- [ ] The first day of summer

100 Things that Make Me Happy (Besides Money)

❑ Running and beating my usual time, distance, or both!

❑ Sunshine on a chilly day

❑ Being captivated by someone beautiful

❑ Sleepovers

❑ Cats in general

❑ Beautifully tended gardens

❑ Swimming on a sweltering hot day

❑ Daydreaming

❑ Being complimented

❑ That feeling of accomplishment you get when you slept through class and didn't get caught

❑ Fireworks

❑ Decorating the Christmas tree

❑ Playing tag

❑ Accomplishing a goal on my life list

❑ Blowing bubbles

❑ Reading my horoscope

❑ Getting a smile from a stranger

❑ Taking a bubble bath in a hotel

❑ Big bookstores

❑ Winning a game I've been playing for a long time

❑ Riding my bike

❑ Snuggling up on cold nights

- [ ] Kicking a pile of autumn leaves
- [ ] Waterfalls
- [ ] Deep, passionate kisses
- [ ] Sticking up for someone who needs it
- [ ] Pictures of my family and friends
- [ ] Flirting
- [ ] Going to the post office
- [ ] The smell after a spring rain shower
- [ ] Candlelight
- [ ] Butterflies
- [ ] Being told I'm loved
- [ ] Finishing a cryptic crossword puzzle
- [ ] Running on the beach on summer nights
- [ ] My birthday
- [ ] Good hair days
- [ ] Being appreciated by my coworkers
- [ ] Swimming when it's raining
- [ ] The smell of freshly mowed grass
- [ ] Small-town parades
- [ ] Shooting stars
- [ ] Deep snow
- [ ] Inspiring quotations
- [ ] Sitting on the roof
- [ ] Playing capture the flag

100 Things that Make Me Happy (Besides Money)

- ☐ Mud wrestling
- ☐ Having someone else make me breakfast
- ☐ Soft breezes
- ☐ Hugs
- ☐ Hot chocolate on a rainy day
- ☐ Bonfires
- ☐ Ladybugs
- ☐ Hearing others laugh
- ☐ The rumbling of thunder on a quiet night
- ☐ Feel-good music turned up to the max
- ☐ Watching the ocean
- ☐ Lavender
- ☐ A view that goes on forever
- ☐ Rainbows
- ☐ Fresh, fluffy, warm towels
- ☐ Eating the produce that I've grown in my very own garden
- ☐ Stars
- ☐ Polka dots
- ☐ Pink sprinkles
- ☐ Outsmarting the teacher
- ☐ Finger painting
- ☐ Autumn bouquets
- ☐ Midnight on New Year's Eve

- ☐ Finding a lucky penny
- ☐ Fat animals like elephants and hippos
- ☐ When someone other than me cleans the bathroom
- ☐ Looking at photo albums
- ☐ Recycling
- ☐ Making compilation CDs for my friends
- ☐ Photo booth pictures
- ☐ Naps
- ☐ Not having to set my alarm clock and sleeping in
- ☐ Fresh linens on the bed
- ☐ Nuzzles from my cat
- ☐ Playing fetch with my dog
- ☐ Meditating
- ☐ Inside jokes
- ☐ The feeling of packing groceries into a reusable shopping bag
- ☐ Walking to dinner with friends
- ☐ Fitting into my jeans from high school
- ☐ Waking up laughing
- ☐ My future
- ☐ Going to church
- ☐ Minimalism

100 Things that Make Me Happy (Besides Money)

- ❏ Realizing things about myself
- ❏ Winter vacation
- ❏ New movies
- ❏ Eskimo kisses
- ❏ Watching people act cute
- ❏ My health
- ❏ Fancy restaurants
- ❏ Mangos and sweet sticky rice
- ❏ Family reunions
- ❏ Fall's changing colors
- ❏ Surprise e-mails from long-lost friends
- ❏ New episodes of my favorite TV shows
- ❏ Moments of inspiration
- ❏ The Rocky Mountains
- ❏ Baseball games
- ❏ Sending birthday cards
- ❏ Fuzzy slippers
- ❏ Warm baths
- ❏ Fresh, hot bread
- ❏ Dark chocolate
- ❏ Someone else taking out the garbage
- ❏ Moonshadows
- ❏ Helping someone
- ❏ Voices of children playing outside at dusk

- ☐ Candles, lots and lots of flickering candles
- ☐ Flannel sheets in the winter
- ☐ Panda cubs
- ☐ Feeling powerful
- ☐ When my husband rubs my feet, shoulders, or back
- ☐ Matinee movies
- ☐ High thread-count sheets
- ☐ Songs that make no sense
- ☐ Sunsets
- ☐ Three-day weekends
- ☐ Sitting in front of a cozy, crackling fire
- ☐ My unconventional collection of keepsakes
- ☐ Hearing real-life inspirational stories
- ☐ Seeing my credit card bills and my debt shrink each month
- ☐ Feeling like a part of a community
- ☐ Two-hour lunches
- ☐ Traditions
- ☐ The smell of fresh coffee
- ☐ Beating my running time
- ☐ Getting a haircut
- ☐ Realizing I don't have to be rich to accomplish my goals

100 Things that Make Me Happy (Besides Money)

- ❏ Sudoku
- ❏ Meat and potatoes
- ❏ Hosting dinner parties
- ❏ Dressing up
- ❏ Being bear hugged so hard that my feet don't touch the floor
- ❏ Making my parents proud
- ❏ Finishing all the chores
- ❏ My husband's unfailing loyalty, compassion, and consideration
- ❏ Watching cartoons and movies from my childhood
- ❏ High heels
- ❏ Getting all A's
- ❏ The feeling after a grueling workout
- ❏ When people admit they were wrong and I was right
- ❏ Celebrating anniversaries
- ❏ Spending the day reading
- ❏ Comedy clubs
- ❏ '80s music
- ❏ Board-game night with friends
- ❏ Picking out the perfect card for someone
- ❏ Falling in love
- ❏ Walking barefoot in the grass

- ☐ Thrift stores
- ☐ Christmas morning
- ☐ Holding hands
- ☐ Cotton candy
- ☐ Acting like a kid again
- ☐ Going to the library and getting new books
- ☐ Relaxing in the hot tub
- ☐ Late-night talks
- ☐ Visiting kittens and puppies at the Humane Society
- ☐ Antique car shows
- ☐ Kissing in the rain
- ☐ Disco balls
- ☐ Learning new things
- ☐ Getting a haircut
- ☐ Meeting interesting people
- ☐ Getting accepted to college
- ☐ Taking photos
- ☐ Trying new recipes
- ☐ My childhood teddy bear
- ☐ The smell of pine needles
- ☐ Walking on the beach and collecting seashells
- ☐ Rereading my favorite books
- ☐ Good dreams

100 Things that Make Me Happy (Besides Money)

- ❑ Surfing
- ❑ Playing tennis
- ❑ A glass of wine after a long day
- ❑ Winning flag football games
- ❑ Nicknames
- ❑ Carving pumpkins
- ❑ Seeing the city lights from a scenic viewing spot
- ❑ Visiting an art museum
- ❑ Weddings
- ❑ Bunny rabbits
- ❑ Being productive
- ❑ Valentines
- ❑ Hiking on a clear day
- ❑ Rosemary
- ❑ Going to yoga every day of the week
- ❑ Bike rides through the country
- ❑ Enjoying beers with friends at our favorite pub
- ❑ Going sailing
- ❑ Laughing babies
- ❑ Trick-or-treating with my kids
- ❑ Painting pictures
- ❑ Laughing until I cry
- ❑ Making a touchdown
- ❑ My college degree

- ❑ Winning free concert tickets on the radio
- ❑ Icicles
- ❑ An empty street at midnight
- ❑ Writing letters on fancy stationery
- ❑ Completing a challenge
- ❑ Leaving work early for the day to enjoy the sunshine
- ❑ British accents
- ❑ Being good at my job
- ❑ Receiving thank-you notes
- ❑ The first crisp fall day
- ❑ Playing the piano
- ❑ Antique music boxes
- ❑ Full moons
- ❑ Sock monkeys
- ❑ Eating fresh, ripe strawberries
- ❑ Relaxing in the sauna at the gym
- ❑ Working in the garden
- ❑ Making snowmen
- ❑ Swimming in the ocean
- ❑ Reading stories to my children
- ❑ Watching babies figure out the world
- ❑ Rummage sales
- ❑ Cashmere scarves

100 Things that Make Me Happy (Besides Money)

- ❏ The first snowfall of the year
- ❏ Peonies
- ❏ Wrapping presents
- ❏ Thunderstorms
- ❏ Road trips with friends
- ❏ An old, torn pair of jeans that I will never part with
- ❏ My mom's home cooking
- ❏ Small dogs
- ❏ Waking up and realizing it's Saturday morning
- ❏ Sitting in a café and reading
- ❏ Winning Monopoly
- ❏ Poetry
- ❏ Children blowing bubbles
- ❏ Renewing my wedding vows
- ❏ Red lipstick
- ❏ Winning prizes and stuffed animals at state fairs
- ❏ Summer vacations
- ❏ Planning trips
- ❏ Fresh pasta
- ❏ Reconnecting with family and friends
- ❏ Discovering new music
- ❏ Really good coffee
- ❏ Hearing a song on the radio I haven't heard in a long time

- ☐ Finishing finals
- ☐ White tiger cubs
- ☐ My favorite sweater
- ☐ Being honestly asked for advice and having the person listen to me
- ☐ Drinking a really cold glass of milk with a peanut butter and jelly sandwich
- ☐ Finishing a marathon
- ☐ The smell of my mom's perfume
- ☐ A walk in a rose garden
- ☐ Blowing out birthday candles
- ☐ Picnics

About the Authors

43Things.com began with three friends who wanted to start a company capable of balancing their life and work pursuits. The Robots (as they call themselves) made lists of their own goals outside of work. When they began comparing their lists of goals, they discovered that sharing their lists was more exciting than the work they were contemplating. And so 43 Things was born.

Lia Steakley is a journalist and a regular contributor to *Seattle Metropolitan* magazine. She has also written for *Wired* and *Business 2.0* magazines and has been a 43 Things member since the beginning.